מגילת השואה

The Shoah Scroll

A Holocaust Liturgy

כנסת הרבנים
**The Rabbinical
Assembly**

מכון שכטר למדעי היהדות
**Schechter Institute
of Jewish Studies**

Jerusalem
2004

First edition: April 2003
Second edition: January 2004

Donors

With gratitude to the donors who made the creation and publication of *Megillat Hashoah* possible.

Chroniclers
Saul and Toba Feldberg
Sam and Gitta Ganz
The Children of Clara and Leslie Reitman,
in their Parents' memory

Scribes
Joe and Phyllis Frieberg
Alex and Genia Grossman
Michael and Marianna Shatz
Barry and Paula Sonshine
Irving and Cathy Stal
Israel and Elena Weinberg

Historians
Abraham and Freda Blankenstein
Leslie and Anna Dan
Alex and Olga Eisen
Harry and Sara Gorman
The Pantirer, Pines and Schwartz Families
Mark and Annette Mincer
David and Felicia Posluns
David and Luba Smuschkowitz
Barry and Nellie Zagdanski
Ian and Sara Zagdanski

Recorders

Ronald and Bunny Appleby
Sidney and Rita Eisen
Sharla Lichtman and Joel Eisen
George and Vera Friedmann
Herbert and Joyce Green
Saul and Evelyn Mintz
Marvin and Pamela Tarek

Witnesses

Israel and Avrum Adler
Coleman and Evelyn Bernstein
Harold and Jeannette Cohen
Samuel and Beverly Cohen
Sydney and Jean Gerstein
Stanley and Sue Goldfarb
Charles and Regina Goldfinger
Pola Goldfluss
Harvey and Jeannette Grossman
Ronald and Heather Hoffman
Bernard and Agnes Klein
Israel Mida and Laurie Walsh
Sol and Cili Neufeld
Les and Eva Saperia
Norman Shelson
Sam and Rose Weisberg
Steeles Memorial Chapel
Dr. Jacob J. Wiener and George Rabner

Committee Members

Megillat Hashoah Committee
Rabbi Prof. David Golinkin, Chair
Rabbi Prof. Reuven Hammer
Rabbi Jules Harlow
Prof. Dalia Ofer
Dr. George Savran
Rabbi Dr. Pesah Schindler
Prof. Avigdor Shinan

Yom Hashoah Liturgy Committee
Rabbi Philip Scheim, Chair
Rabbi Dr. Jeffrey Hoffman
Rabbi Dr. Avram Reisner
Mr. Larry Rosenberg
Rabbi Joel Meyers, Ex Officio

Megillat Hashoah Project
Mr. Alex Eisen, Chair
Rabbi Philip Scheim, Co-Chair

Editors
Rabbi Prof. David Golinkin
Rabbi Philip Scheim

Contents

The publication of *Megillat Hashoah* marks a milestone in the transformation of *Yom Hashoah* into a sacred day within the cycle of the Jewish year, taking its rightful place as a day of mourning and religious commemoration. As early as the late 1960s, I called upon the Rabbinical Assembly to begin the work needed to make this day one that would be observed in appropriate ways by every synagogue and, indeed, by every individual Jew. My feeling then, as now, was that unless *Yom Hashoah* is marked by appropriate liturgical formulations within the *Siddur* to be recited on 27 Nissan, it would not outlast the lives of those who experienced the horrors of the *Shoah*. In the 1980s, the Rabbinical Assembly of Israel pioneered this effort by issuing a *Siddur* for *Yom Hashoah,* which was later incorporated into *Siddur Va-ani Tefilati*. The Rabbinical Assembly's new edition of *Siddur Sim Shalom* contains a slightly revised version of that service. *Megillat Hashoah* now caps that endeavor by supplying us with a Hebrew text with translation, which will be read at services on *Yom Hashoah* year after year, a text that tells the story of the *Shoah* in brief but powerful passages that can and must become part of the collective memory of the Jewish people. This repetition, year after year, from generation to generation, will become the liturgical foundation for commemoration of these terrible events that must never be forgotten. Of course, these brief chapters cannot and are not intended to tell the whole story, but they can serve as a goad to learn more and more. *Yom Hashoah* now has its own *megillah*. Having one central text, shared by Jews wherever they live, will unite us and make possible the perpetuation of the story. It will help us to fulfill what has become the new imperative of Jewish life: We must all view ourselves as if we had personally experienced the *Shoah*. The emphasis here is on the words "as if", since no one who was not there can possibly understand what it was like, though we can identify with them and their suffering.

As one who lived in the United States and was as far from the *Shoah* as one could be, it is paradoxical that I have always felt compelled to contrast my life with that of those in Europe, and in that way to identify with them. I was born the year that Hitler came to power. When I was a young child, the Nazi persecution of the Jews began and laws were promulgated against my people. I started school when *Kristalnacht* took place. I was studying in the United States together with children of different races and religions when Jews in Germany were being prevented from attending German schools and when concentration camps were being built. I had not yet reached the age of Bar Mitzvah when ghettos were created throughout Europe and children younger than I were scratching through garbage heaps to find a scrap of food and Jews were being slaughtered in Nazi gas chambers and shot at the edge of mass graves throughout eastern Europe. By the time of my Bar Mitzvah, it was all over – men, women and children had been annihilated in numbers humanity had never experienced before. Nothing stood between me and the *Shoah* but the fateful decision of my grandparents to leave Europe and come to America at the beginning of the twentieth century. All of us were potential victims of the *Shoah* and we must never forget that.

The *Shoah* arouses feelings within us that are difficult to bear and questions to which we have no answers. It demands a response, but it is difficult to know how to respond. We want to understand, but there is no possibility of understanding. It challenges our faith in God, in religion and, most of all, our faith in humanity. Centuries ago our Sages had no answer to the question: why was Cain permitted to kill Abel? In a daring midrash based on the verse "The voice of your brother's blood cries out to Me from the ground" (Genesis 4:10), Rabbi Shimon bar Yohai told this parable: It may be likened to two gladiators striving with one another before the emperor. If the emperor wished, he could have separated them. But he did not wish to do so, so one overpowered the other and killed him. As he was being slain, the gladiator cried out, "I demand justice from the Emperor!" Thus, "The sound of your brother's blood cries out to Me from the ground!" (Genesis Rabbah 22).

The voices of six million cry out before God for justice. We have no answer but the sound of silence. And yet we must never say or teach that the *Shoah* represented the will of God, that the *Shoah* was God's punishment, or that it was justified because it was followed so soon by the creation of the State of Israel. We may not have answers to the mysteries of the *Shoah,* but there are some answers that must be rejected completely for the honor of our people and for the honor of God. Such thoughts stand in complete contrast to Judaism's teaching that God is the God of mercy and righteousness. As Abraham Joshua Heschel once remarked, "History is the arena in which the will of God is defied". It is the place where God commands us to respect and even to love other human beings, and yet Cain slays Abel. Such a slaying is in complete contradiction to God's express desires, but is consistent with the fact that we are all granted free will.

Regarding the enslavement of the Israelites in Egypt, the rabbis taught that when we were enslaved, God too was enslaved – as it were – and was freed only when Israel was redeemed (see *Mekhilta Pisha* 14). So too we can say that when Israel was sent to the camps and the gas chambers, the Holy One was with them. God identifies with those who suffer, with the persecuted, not with the persecutors. We may not have the answers, but at least we can tell the story.

With the publication of *Megillat Hashoah* we express the depth of our mourning for our brothers and sisters who were destroyed in this terrible Holocaust. We pledge ourselves to keep their memories alive forever and to dedicate ourselves to the proposition that *Am Yisrael Hai* – we shall continue to live and to proclaim the greatness of the Jewish people and its way of life.

Rabbi Reuven Hammer
President, The Rabbinical Assembly
Jerusalem
Kristalnacht 5763

The Jewish people is an *am olam*, an eternal people, with a historic memory thousands of years old. It has always succeeded in commemorating major historic events with the aid of religious rituals.

When David Ben-Gurion appeared before the UN Commission Regarding the Partition of Palestine in the summer of 1947, he said:

> About 300 years ago a ship named the "Mayflower" set sail to the New World. It was an important event in the annals of England and America. Yet I wonder if there is even one Englishman who knows exactly when that ship set sail, and how many Americans know how many people were on that ship? And what type of bread did they eat when they left England? And yet, more than 3,300 years ago, before the Mayflower set sail, the Jews left Egypt. And every Jew in the world – even in America and Soviet Russia – knows *exactly* on which day they left: on the 15th of Nissan. And everyone knows *exactly* what kind of bread the Jews ate: *matzot.* And until today Jews all over the world eat this *matzah* on the 15th of Nissan – in America, in Russia and in other countries – and... recount the Exodus... And they open [the *Seder*] with two statements: "This year slaves, next year free men; this year here, next year in Eretz Yisrael". This is the nature of the Jews. (Noam Zion and David Dishon, *A Different Night*, 1997, p. 39)

In other words, Ben-Gurion emphasized that on Pesah we *remember* the Exodus from Egypt by a *religious act* – the *Seder* – in order to remember and to relive the Exodus once a year. As a result, every Jew in the world is well-versed in this seminal episode in the history of our people.

The same applies to the Destruction of the Temple. As we learn in the tractate of *Bava Batra* (fol. 60b):

> ...The Sages said: A man plasters his house and leaves a little bare... a man prepares a festive meal and leaves out one small portion... a woman puts on all her jewelry and leaves off one small item... as it is written: "If I forget you, O Jerusalem, let my right hand wither. Let my tongue stick to my palate if I do not remember you, if I do not keep Jerusalem in mind even at my happiest hour" (*Psalms* 137:5-6). ... What is meant by "my happiest hour"? Rabbi Isaac said: this is symbolized by the burnt ashes, which we place on the head of a bridegroom...

This passage was codified by Maimonides and the Shulhan Arukh and these practices were actually followed by many Jewish communities throughout the Diaspora. Similarly, since the fourteenth century we break a glass under the wedding canopy in order to commemorate the Destruction of Jerusalem at our happiest moments (*Kol Bo, Hilkhot Ta'anit*, 25d and *Minhagey d'vey Maharam*, p. 82).

In other words, we remembered the victory of the Exodus through *religious acts*; and the failure of the Destruction of the Temple through *religious acts*.

Indeed, tragedies which befell our people were remembered in three different ways:

First of all, we decreed public fast days. In addition to Tisha B'Av and the other fast days connected to the Destruction of the Temple, we decreed public fast days in order to commemorate other disasters.

For example, on the 23rd of Shvat, January 18, 749 a terrible earthquake struck the Land of Israel, destroying many cities and killing thousands of Jews and Arabs. We learn from a *genizah* fragment of a *Siddur* from Eretz Yisrael that the 23rd of Shvat was declared a *Ta'anit Tzibbur* (public fast day) which was observed in *Eretz Yisrael* for hundreds of years (*Tarbitz* 29 [5720], pp. 339-344).

On the 20th day of Sivan, 4931 (May 26, 1171), thirty-two Jews were burned at the stake in Blois, France, as a result of a blood libel, the first in continental Europe. As a result, the

> 20th of Sivan, 4931, was accepted voluntarily by all the communities of France, the English Isles, and the Rhineland, as a day of mourning and fasting. This was also the command of Rabbeinu Tam, who wrote letters informing them that it was proper to fix this day as a fast for all our people and that this fast must be greater than the Fast of Gedaliah... (A.M. Haberman, *Sefer Gezeirot Ashkenaz V'zarefat*, Jerusalem, 1945, p. 126)

Exactly 477 years later, a Jewish tragedy of much greater proportions began in Poland. On the 20th of Sivan, 5408 (June 10, 1648) Bogdan Chmielnicki and his pillaging Cossacks destroyed the flourishing Jewish community of Nemirov, Poland. During the course of the next six months, these mobs wantonly tortured and murdered approximately 50,000 innocent Jews and destroyed a large number of Jewish communities. In 1650, the Council of Four Lands

> decreed a public fast day on the 20th of Sivan for the entire kingdom of Poland for generations, on the very day on which... the massacre of Nemirov occurred. That was the first community which died for the Sanctification of God's name... (*Y'vein Metzulah*, ed. Halprin, 5726, p. 78).

Indeed, this is the reason that a group of teachers and students at the Schechter Institute hold a public fast day every year on *Yom Hashoah*.

Second, we have remembered tragedies by designating periods of mourning on the Hebrew calendar, such as the Three Weeks between the 17th of Tammuz and Tisha B'av and the Sefirah Season between Pesah and Shavuot.

Third, we have composed *megillot* (scrolls) and *kinot* (elegies). For example, *Megillat Eikhah* (the Scroll of Lamentations) commemorates the Destruction of the First

Temple. The great earthquake in the year 749 was commemorated in a series of liturgical poems. The blood libel of 1171 was commemorated by liturgical poems and chronicles. And the well-known *posek* (halakhic authority), Rabbi Shabetai Hacohen, the Shakh (1621-1662), composed a scroll named *Megillat Afa* (see *Zekhariah* 5:1-2) as well as elegies about the massacres of 1648-1649, which were printed in Amsterdam in 1651. Those elegies and others, reprinted many times, were recited in Eastern Europe on the 20th of Sivan for 300 years until the Holocaust.

Indeed, some writers have suggested writing a *megillah* in order to commemorate the Shoah. In 1970, Binyamin West wrote: "I wish to suggest to the Yad Vashem directorate that it announce a prize for a scroll of the Holocaust. We need an *Eikhah* of the Holocaust, something short and strong, that will have an effect on believers and non-believers alike" (*Yad Vashem News* 2 [1970], p. 7).

In 1981, Rabbi Meir Amsel, a Haredi rabbi and Holocaust survivor, published an article in *Hamaor* (Vol. 33 [Sivan-Tammuz 5741], p. 17) where he stated:

> Therefore, now that it is 36 years after the terrible disaster, the leaders of the people, the *admorim* (Hassidic rabbis) and the rabbis should gather together with the heads of *Yeshivot*, to confer and to set a fast day, to lament and to eulogize the great destruction which happened to the people of Israel ...*and to enact a megillah like the Scroll of Eikhah*, that will be read on this day, and to transmit it to future generations, until the arrival of the Messiah who will avenge the blood of our slain brethren.*

Megillat Hashoah – The Shoah Scroll – fills the need described by Rabbi Amsel. But, you may ask, why do we

---

* Regarding all of the above, see David Golinkin, *Conservative Judaism* 37/4 (Summer 1984), pp. 52-64 and *Eit La'asot* 3 (Summer 5751), pp. 37-54.

need to compose a Shoah Scroll right *now*? There are three answers to this question:

First of all, the survivors are disappearing, and with them the living testimonies. Rabbi Pesach Schindler, one of our committee members, is a survivor. Prof. Avigdor Shinan – the author of the scroll – is the son and nephew of survivors. Dr. George Savran is the son-in-law of survivors. I am the nephew of survivors. But in one generation's time, no survivors or children of survivors will remain to testify about what happened. We must determine the methods of commemoration *now*, when there is still a living connection to the *Shoah*.

Second, as already mentioned, historic events are remembered in Judaism only if it they are anchored in *religious* rituals. The kindling of six torches by survivors in the courtyard of Yad Vashem is a meaningful ritual, but will it last when there are no living survivors?

Third, we are witnessing a growing phenomenon of Holocaust deniers. Therefore, it is our difficult mission to educate our children and the whole world about the Holocaust, a unique event in the history of mankind.

We hope that this scroll will be accepted by *Klal Yisrael* (the collective Jewish people) as a meaningful religious way to commemorate the memory of the Holocaust for generations, just as we were successful in commemorating the Exodus, on the one hand, and the Destruction of the Temple, on the other. If we succeed, we shall have fulfilled the adage attributed to the Ba'al Shem-Tov:

הגולה נמשכה מהשכחה, ובזכירה סוד הגאולה

The Diaspora was prolonged by forgetfulness,
and remembrance is the secret of redemption.

Rabbi David Golinkin
President, The Schechter Institute
Jerusalem
Kristalnacht 5763

L oss of memory is scary whenever and to whomever it occurs. But to Jews – in particular, to Jews of our times – it is terrifying. We have a great deal to remember, including memories that the rest of the world would rather see forgotten. We fear for ourselves when we realize that each year to come means fewer survivors of the Holocaust left to remind us and the world of what happened, of what human beings are capable of doing to each other. We fear for the millions who will be wiped out of all earthly record, if not for our determined effort to insure that they are remembered and revered until the end of time.

We know that the memories of the previous generation which the next generation carries into the future are imperfect at best. They are a mere echo of the events, times, feelings and conditions described. This is all the more reason for us to listen as well as we can to the witnesses of events that preceded us, for in the next generation, it is we who become witnesses to the witnesses. It is our testimony, one, two or ten generations removed from actual events, that will help set the tone of the Jewish future.

The Jewish calendar has aided our memory process throughout our long history. *Sukkot* commemorates our ancient wilderness wandering, following the Exodus from Egypt, which we remember through the *Pesah* festival. *Shavuot* reminds us of the Sinai Revelation of Torah. *Hanukah* and *Purim* commemorate the Hasmonean victory over the Hellenist assimilationists and the Greek-Syrian Empire, and our being saved from evil intent in ancient Persia. Fast days along the map of our calendar remind us of the various stages in the Destructions of the Ancient Temple in Jerusalem.

Remembering the Holocaust, though, has been challenging, on a religious level. It is relatively so soon after the events, that we have not yet even come close to uniformity as a people, in figuring out how to put our memorializing the Six Million into a religious context.

Several years ago, Alex Eisen, a prominent member of the Toronto community and of my congregation, and a Holocaust survivor, raised the idea of producing a Megillah to be read on Yom Hashoah, just as *Eikhah* is read on *Tisha B'Av,* and *Esther* on *Purim.* He felt, correctly, that a consistent approach to *Yom Hashoah* was necessary, that a *Megillah,* to be read in synagogue on *Yom Hashoah,* would provide the day a unifying structure, and lead to *Yom Hashoah* being observed by more Jews and more Jewish communities, in a serious spiritual way.

Not long after Alex proposed the *Megillah,* I brought the idea to Rabbi Seymour L. Essrog ל״ז, then President, and Rabbi Joel Meyers, Executive Vice-President of the Rabbinical Assembly, both of whom warmly endorsed the project. All that remained was the writing of the project, an effort which was aided by a happy coincidence. For many years, Rabbi David Golinkin, President of the Schechter Institute in Jerusalem, has served as Auxiliary High Holiday Rabbi of Beth David B'nai Israel Beth Am, my congregation, and has been hosted by Alex Eisen. Alex discussed the idea with Rabbi Golinkin, leading the Schechter Institute to become an active partner in the project with the Rabbinical Assembly. It was under Rabbi Golinkin's guidance that the final document came to be, written in a magnificent Hebrew by Professor Avigdor Shinan, and beautifully translated into English by Rabbi Jules Harlow. Ms. Tova Strauss corrected the vocalization and supplied the cantillation. Mr. Donny Finkel of Leshon Limudim Ltd. typeset the book and saw it through the press.

Megillat Hashoah would not have achieved fruition, were it not for the tireless fundraising efforts of Alex Eisen, and the generosity of donors acknowledged elsewhere in this booklet.

Remembering the Six Million needs to enter the synagogue in a structured and consistent manner. It is our hope that *Megillat Hashoah* will be read on *Yom Hashoah* every year in synagogues and communities throughout the world.

It is through the perspective of memory, both immediate and ancient, that we are better able to prepare ourselves for the challenge of a vibrant Jewish future. May we prove equal to the challenge of transmitting those memories into tomorrow's world.

Rabbi Philip S. Scheim
Toronto, Ontario
Kristalnacht 5763

סֵדֶר תְּפִלָּה לְעֶרֶב יוֹם הַשּׁוֹאָה

מתפללים תפילת מנחה.

אֲרוֹן הַתּוֹרָה, אֲרוֹן הָאֱמוּנָה, עוֹמֵד בּוֹדֵד שָׁכוּל.

בָּאנוּ לִזְכּוֹר אֶת אֵלֶּה שֶׁאֵין לְשַׁכְּחָם.

בָּאנוּ לְדַבֵּר עַל דָּבָר שֶׁאִי אֶפְשָׁר לְדַבֵּר,
אֲבָל אֵין לְהַשְׁאִירוֹ בִּלְתִּי נֶאֱמָר.

בָּאנוּ לְהַזְכִּיר לְעַצְמֵנוּ אֶת אֲשֶׁר נַעֲשָׂה
וְאֶת אֲשֶׁר לֹא נַעֲשָׂה.

בָּאנוּ לִשְׁאֹל אֶת הַשְּׁאֵלוֹת שֶׁאֵין לָהֶן מַעֲנֶה -
אֲבָל אֵין לְהַשְׁאִירָן לְלֹא שְׁאֵלָה.

יוֹדְעִים אָנוּ כֵּיצַד לִזְכּוֹר אֶת אֵלֶּה שֶׁהִכַּרְנוּ וְאֵינָם.

יוֹדְעִים אָנוּ לְהַעֲלוֹת זִכְרוֹ שֶׁל אָדָם אֶחָד.

אֲבָל כֻּלָּנוּ אֲבֵלִים, כֻּלָּנוּ מַעֲלִים זִכְרָם
שֶׁל שֵׁשׁ מֵאוֹת רִבּוֹא - וְלֹא רַק שֶׁל אֶחָד בִּלְבָד

לֹא רַק אֵלֶּה שֶׁהִכַּרְנוּ,
אֶלָּא אֵלֶּה שֶׁאִישׁ אֵינוֹ מַכִּירָם...

הרב ראובן המר

Commemorative Ritual for Yom Hashoah Eve

The Service begins with the recitation of *Minhah*.

The ark of Torah, of faith, of learning,
stands empty and bereft.

We have come here to remember
those who cannot be forgotten.

We have come to speak of that which cannot be spoken
but must not be left unsaid.

We have come to remind not others but ourselves
of what was done and what was not done.

We have come to ask questions that cannot be answered
but cannot be left unasked.

We know how to remember the dead we have known.

We know how to commemorate the death of one person.

But all of us are mourners;
all of us recall not one but six million ones.

Not only those we have known,
but those no one can know,
the names that are forever lost.

Rabbi Reuven Hammer

שׁוֹמֵר יִשְׂרָאֵל,

שְׁמֹר שְׁאֵרִית יִשְׂרָאֵל,

וְאַל יֹאבַד יִשְׂרָאֵל

הָאוֹמְרִים: שְׁמַע יִשְׂרָאֵל.

שׁוֹמֵר גּוֹי אֶחָד,

שְׁמֹר שְׁאֵרִית עַם אֶחָד,

וְאַל יֹאבַד גּוֹי אֶחָד

הַמְיַחֲדִים שִׁמְךָ יְיָ אֱלֹהֵינוּ יְיָ אֶחָד.

שׁוֹמֵר גּוֹי קָדוֹשׁ,

שְׁמֹר שְׁאֵרִית עַם קָדוֹשׁ,

וְאַל יֹאבַד גּוֹי קָדוֹשׁ

הַמְשַׁלְּשִׁים בְּשָׁלֹשׁ קְדֻשּׁוֹת לְקָדוֹשׁ.

מִתְרַצֶּה בְּרַחֲמִים וּמִתְפַּיֵּס בְּתַחֲנוּנִים,

הִתְרַצֵּה וְהִתְפַּיֵּס לְדוֹר עָנִי כִּי אֵין עוֹזֵר.

יָשַׁבְנוּ גַם בָּכִינוּ בְּזָכְרֵנוּ אֶת אַחֵינוּ

שֶׁנִּטְבְּחוּ וְשֶׁנִּשְׂרְפוּ וְשֶׁנֶּחְנְקוּ בִּימֵי עָנְיֵנוּ.

אָבִינוּ מַלְכֵּנוּ,

חָנֵּנוּ וַעֲנֵנוּ כִּי אֵין בָּנוּ מַעֲשִׂים.

עֲשֵׂה עִמָּנוּ צְדָקָה וָחֶסֶד וְהוֹשִׁיעֵנוּ.

Guardian of Israel,
guard the remnant of Israel;

and preserve the people Israel, who proclaim:
Sh'ma Yisrael.

Guardian of a unique people,
guard the remnant of that people;

and preserve that people who affirm:
Adonai is our God, *Adonai* alone.

Guardian of a holy people,
guard the remnant of that holy people;

and preserve that holy people
who chant in praise of the Holy One:
Kadosh, Kadosh, Kadosh.

O God, moved by prayer and reconciled by supplication,

accept the prayers amid the supplication of our
afflicted generation, for there is no one else to help.

We have sat and wept as we recalled our kin

who were slaughtered, suffocated and burned to ashes
in the time of our deepest distress.

Avinu Malkenu,
have mercy on us and answer us,
for we are devoid of good deeds.

Treat us with mercy and kindness, and save us.

The *Ma'ariv* Service is recited.   מתפללים תפילת מעריב.

Megilat Hashoah, The Shoah Scroll may be read at this time. The lighting of six candles may take place before reading the Megillah, or one candle may be lit at the conclusion of each of the six chapters of Megillat Hashoah. Ani Ma'amin may be sung or the melody played during the candle-lighting.

Ani Ma'amin   אֲנִי מַאֲמִין

I believe   אֲנִי מַאֲמִין

with perfect faith   בֶּאֱמוּנָה שְׁלֵמָה

In the coming of the Messiah,   בְּבִיאַת הַמָּשִׁיחַ

I believe.   אֲנִי מַאֲמִין

And even though he may tarry   וְאַף עַל פִּי שֶׁיִּתְמַהְמֵהַּ

Nonetheless, do I believe.   עִם כָּל זֶה אֲנִי מַאֲמִין.

The Shoah Scroll

מְגִלַּת הַשּׁוֹאָה

מאת אביגדור שנאן

by Avigdor Shinan

translated from the Hebrew by Jules Harlow

פרק א

רֵאשִׁית דָּבָר

1 אָמַר כּוֹתֵב דִּבְרֵי הַיָּמִים:

2 אֲרֻכּוֹת הֵן תּוֹלְדוֹתָיו שֶׁל עַם־עוֹלָם, אַלְפֵי שָׁנִים, וּבָהֶן
שְׁנוֹת טוֹבָה וּשְׁנוֹת רָעָה, שָׁנִים שְׁלֵווֹת וְשָׁנִים אֲיֻמּוֹת:

3 בְּאַרְצוֹ וּבְגֵכָר, בֵּין הָאֻמּוֹת וּכְעַם חָפְשִׁי, זָכָה לְיָמִים רַבִּים
שֶׁל נַחַת, וּבְמַהֲלָכָן תָּרַם מִכּוֹחוֹתָיו לְאֶחָיו בְּנֵי הָאָדָם,
וְהֶעֱנִיק לָהֶם אֶת הָאֱמוּנָה בְּאֵל אֶחָד וְאֶת יוֹם הַשַּׁבָּת, אֶת
סֵפֶר הַסְּפָרִים וְאֶת מוּסַר הַנְּבִיאִים:

4 אַךְ בְּיָמִים אֲחֵרִים,
קָשִׁים וַחֲשׁוּכִים, נֶאֱנַק תַּחַת עֹל שֶׁל כּוֹבְשִׁים
וּמְשַׁעְבְּדִים: נַפְשׁוֹ עֻנְּתָה בְּמִלְחֲמוֹת דָּת וּגְזֵרוֹת, שְׂרֵפוֹת

5 עַל הַמּוֹקֵד, דְּחִיקָה לְגֶטָאוֹת, פּוֹגְרוֹמִים וַעֲלִילוֹת דָּם,

6 גֵּרוּשִׁים וְגָלֻיּוֹת, הַשְׁפָּלָה וְלַעַג: לֹא שָׁקַט הָעָם וְלֹא שָׁלֵו,
וּמִפְלֶצֶת שִׂנְאַת יִשְׂרָאֵל פָּעֲרָה שׁוּב וָשׁוּב אֶת פִּיהָ וְעָמְדָה

7 עָלָיו בְּכָל דּוֹר וָדוֹר לְכַלּוֹתוֹ: וְעִם כָּל זֹאת חָרַק הָעָם אֶת
שִׁנָּיו, הִצְדִּיק עָלָיו אֶת הַדִּין, נָתַן גֵּוֹו לַמַּכִּים, וּפְעָמִים אַף
פָּשַׁט אֶת צַוָּארוֹ עַל גַּבֵּי הַמִּזְבֵּחַ, נָדַד וְנִרְדַּף וְתָר לוֹ
מְקוֹם מִקְלָט עַד יַעֲבֹר זָעַם:

CHAPTER I

IN THE BEGINNING

1 So spoke the Chronicler:

2 Long is the history of the eternal people, extending for millennia, including good years and bad years, tranquil

3 years and dreadful years. In its own land and in Diaspora lands, among the nations and as a free people, it enjoyed long periods of repose during which it contributed of its endowments to fellow mortals, bestowing upon them the Sabbath and faith in one God, the Book of books and the teachings of the

4 prophets. At times, however, in darkened and difficult days, it struggled under the burdens imposed by

5 vanquishers and subjugators. It was afflicted, body and soul, by religious wars and persecutions, burnings at the stake and being crowded into ghettos, blood libels and pogroms, expulsions and exiles, degradation

6 and derision. The people had neither serenity nor tranquility; and the monster of Jew-hatred again and again threatened to swallow it whole, rose up against it

7 in every generation attempting to destroy it. Nevertheless, the people gritted its teeth, accepted the heavenly judgment and, groaning, even at times stretched its neck on the sacrificial altar. Homeless and hunted, it sought a safe haven, a refuge for resting a while until the time of wrath had passed.

[מכאן ועד סוף הפרק יש לקרוא במנגינת "איכה".]

8 אַךְ מַה־שֶּׁאֲרַע־לּוֹ לְעַם יִשְׂרָאֵל בְּאֵירוֹפָּה הַנָּאצִית, אֵין לוֹ
שֵׁם וּמַה־שֶּׁעָלְתָה לְבָנָיו וְלִבְנוֹתָיו אִי־אֶפְשָׁר לַפֶּה
9 לְפָרְשׁוֹ: אֵין־סְפֹר בְּנֵי־אָדָם הָגְלוּ מִבָּתֵּיהֶם נִקְרְעוּ
10 מִמִּשְׁפְּחוֹתֵיהֶם הֻשְׁפְּלוּ עַד־עָפָר וְשֻׁעְבְּדוּ עַד־מָוֶת: שִׁשָּׁה
מִלְיוֹן בְּרוּאִים בְּצֶלֶם נֶחְנְקוּ נִשְׂרְפוּ אוֹ נוֹרוּ נִקְבְּרוּ חַיִּים
11 אוֹ־מֵתוּ בְּרָעָב בַּצָּמָא וּבַקֹּר: הַפַּעַם פָּעֲרָה הַמִּפְלֶצֶת
אֶת־פִּיהָ לִבְלִי חֹק בְּצוּחָתָהּ מַקְפִּיאָה דָם וּבִקְשָׁה לַעֲקֹר
12 אֶת־הַכֹּל: בְּלֹא רַחֵם יָצְאָה לְהַשְׁמִיד לַהֲרֹג וּלְאַבֵּד
אֶת־הָעָם כֻּלּוֹ מִן־הַבָּאִים בַּיָּמִים וְעַד לְעֻבָּרִים שֶׁבְּמֵעֵי
13 אִמּוֹתֵיהֶם: רַכָּבוֹת אֵין־סְפֹר דָּהֲרוּ דְחוּסוֹת אֶל־הַמַּחֲנוֹת
וַעֲשַׁן הָאֲרֻבּוֹת הִתַּמֵּר אֶל־הָאֱלֹהִים אַךְ הַשָּׁמַיִם הָיוּ
14 נְחֹשֶׁת וְהָרָקִיעַ בַּרְזֶל: שְׁקְשׁוּק גַּלְגַּלֵּי הַקְּרוֹנוֹת הִתְעָרֵב
בִּנְבִיחוֹת הַכְּלָבִים וְאֶל־טְרִיקַת דַּלְתוֹת הַבַּרְזֶל הִצְטָרֵף
15 רַעַשׁ הַנְּעָלַיִם הַמְּסֻמָּרוֹת: כִּתְזַמֶּרֶת עֲנָק דּוֹרְסָנִית
הֶחֱרִישׁוּ כָּל־אֵלֶּה אֶת קוֹל הַדְּמָמָה הַדַּקָּה אֲשֶׁר בָּקַע
מִלְּבּוֹת מְתֵי הַמְעַט חֲסִידֵי אֻמּוֹת הָעוֹלָם אֲשֶׁר־נָגַע בָּהֶם
16 דְּבַר הָאֱלֹהִים: זְכָרָה לָהֶם | אֱלֹהִים זֹאת לְטוֹבָה:
17 הַרְבֵּה כְּבָר רָאִיתִי וְהַרְבֵּה עוֹד אֶרְאֶה אַךְ מַה־שֶּׁנִּגְלָה
18 לְעֵינַי שָׁם לֹא אוּכַל לָשׁוּב וְלִרְאוֹת: כָּל־הַמִּלִּים שֶׁנִּבְרְאוּ
וְשֶׁיִּבָּרְאוּ בְּכָל־הַשָּׂפוֹת כֻּלָּן לֹא־יַצְלִיחוּ לְתָאֵר וְלוּ מְעַט
19 מִמַּה־שֶּׁנִּגְלָה לְעֵינָי: וְאַף זֹאת אֵדַע לֹא אוּכַל לִשְׁכַּח
וְלֹא־יִהְיֶה־בִּי הַכֹּחַ לְהָבִין:

[From here to the end of the chapter is chanted in the mode of *Eikhah*.]

8   What befell the people Israel in Nazi Europe, however, is beyond classification, and what confronted its sons
9   and daughters defies description. Untold numbers were forced out of their homes, torn from their families,
10   trampled in the dust, worked to death. Six million created in the divine image were strangled, cremated, shot, buried alive; they died of starvation, of thirst, and
11   of the cold. This time the monster stretched open its mouth beyond bounds, with a blood-curdling shriek and with stinking breath, and sought to eradicate
12   everything. Without mercy it set out to destroy, to slaughter, and to lay waste the entire people, from those nearing the end of their days to embryos in their
13   mothers' wombs. Countless trains stuffed with human cargo sped to the camps, where from chimneys smoke ascended to God; but the heavens were brass and the
14   firmament iron. The click-clack of boxcar wheels blended with the barking of dogs, and the clank of iron doors merged with the stomping of hobnailed
15   boots. Like a gigantic thundering orchestra, all of these sounds silenced the thin, small voice bursting out of the hearts of the precious few, the righteous of the world's nations who had been touched by the word of God.
16   May God recall their deeds in their favor.
17   So much have I seen and so much have I yet to see, but what was revealed to me there I never could see again.
18   All of the words in the world, created and yet to be created, in every single language, will never be able to describe even a small part of what was displayed before
19   my eyes. And this too do I know: Never will I be able to forget, and never will I have the power to understand.

פֶּרֶק ב

מְלֹא כָל־הָאָרֶץ "תֹּהוּ וָבֹהוּ

1 מִתּוֹךְ יוֹמָן מַסָּע אֶל עוֹלָם אַחֵר:

2 חָבֵר הָיִיתִי בַּמִּשְׁלַחַת הַקְּטַנָּה שֶׁל עִתּוֹנָאִים אֲשֶׁר

הִתְגַּנְּבָה אֶל הַגֶּטוֹ כְּדֵי לִרְאוֹת מַה מִּתְרַחֵשׁ מֵאֲחוֹרֵי

3 חוֹמוֹתָיו: שְׁמֹנֶה שָׁעוֹת שֶׁהָיִיתִי שָׁם וּבָהֶן זָקַנְתִּי בְּעֶשֶׂר

4 שָׁנִים: בְּדַרְכֵּנוּ עָצַרְנוּ לְהִתְפַּלֵּל בַּכְּנֵסִיָּה, שֶׁהֲרֵי הָיָה זֶה

5 יוֹם רִאשׁוֹן: כְּשֶׁנָּדַם אַחֲרוֹן צְלִילָיו שֶׁל הָעוּגָב הֶאֱזַנּוּ

6 לְדִבְרֵי הַכֹּמֶר: הוּא דִּבֵּר עַל יִסּוּרִים וָסֵבֶל, עַל אַהֲבָה

וְרַחֲמִים, חֶמְלָה וָחֶסֶד, וְשִׁלַּח אִתָּנוּ לְדַרְכֵּנוּ בְּבִרְכַּת "יְהִי

7 הָאֱלֹהִים עִמָּכֶם": אַךְ כְּשֶׁחָלַפְנוּ עַל פְּנֵי בֵּיתָנֵי הַשְּׁמִירָה

אֲשֶׁר בַּחוֹמָה הַמַּקִּיפָה אֶת הַגֶּטוֹ, נוֹתְרוּ עִמָּנוּ הַיִּסּוּרִים

וְהַסֵּבֶל, וְהֵם בִּלְבַד:

8 עִם כְּנִיסָתֵנוּ יָצְאָה לְמוּלֵנוּ עֲגָלָה וּשְׁלֹשָׁה אֲנָשִׁים מוֹשְׁכִים

9 דּוֹחֲפִים אוֹתָהּ: גּוּיוֹת גְּרוּמוֹת נֶעֶרְמוּ עָלֶיהָ, רֹאשָׁן

הַמְּטֻלְטָל בְּקֶצֶב מַהֲמוּרוֹת הַכְּבִישׁ כְּאִלּוּ נָד לָנוּ לְשָׁלוֹם:

10 כָּךְ נִפְגַּשְׁנוּ לָרִאשׁוֹנָה עִם בֶּן בְּרִיתוֹ שֶׁל הַמָּוֶת, עִם

11 הָרָעָב: אִי אֶפְשָׁר הָיָה שֶׁלֹּא לָחוּשׁ בּוֹ בְּכָל פִּנָּה, וְהוּא

שֶׁהִגְנִיעַ בְּלֹא תַכְלִית נְחִילֵי אָדָם בָּרְחוֹבוֹת, חֲסַר אוֹנִים

12 וְיֵאוּשׁ עַל פְּנֵיהֶם: וּבְכָל אֲשֶׁר תַּבִּיט מַרְאוֹת פְּלָצוּת:

גּוּפַת מֵת, פָּנֶיהָ מְכֻסִּים בְּעִתּוֹן, וְגֶבֶר מֵסִיר בְּחִפָּזוֹן אֶת

הַמְּעִיל אֲשֶׁר עָלֶיהָ וּמְחַטֵּט בְּכִיסֶיהָ בְּתִקְוָה; יַלְדָּה

CHAPTER II

THE EARTH IS FILLED
WITH CHAOS AND CONFUSION

1   From the journal of a journey to another world:

2   I was part of a small delegation of journalists that stole into the ghetto in order to see what was happening

3   behind its walls. I stayed there for eight hours, during

4   which I aged ten years. On our way there, we stopped

5   at a church to worship, since it was Sunday. When the last notes of the organ had faded, we listened to the

6   words of the priest. He spoke of suffering and affliction, of love and compassion, of pity and kindness, and sent us on our way with the blessing, "May God be with

7   you." But when we passed the guardhouses placed in the wall surrounding the ghetto, we were left with the suffering and the affliction, them alone.

8   As we entered, a cart was coming toward us, pushed

9   and pulled by three men. Bloated corpses were heaped upon it, their heads bouncing to a rhythm determined by muddy ruts in the road, as if they were greeting us.

10   Thus for the first time we met death's partner, famine.

11   It was impossible not to feel its presence in every corner, and it was the force endlessly propelling streams of weakened people through the streets, their

12   faces filled with despair. Wherever you looked, terrifying sights: a dead body, its face covered by a newspaper, and a man hastily removing its overcoat while digging in its pockets with anticipation; a young

וּבְחֵיקָהּ אֲחוֹתָהּ הַתִּינֹקֶת הַמְיֻבֶּבֶת בִּרְעָבוֹנָהּ בְּאֶפֶס
כּוֹחוֹת, סָפֵק גּוֹסֶסֶת סָפֵק יְשֵׁנָה; יֵשׁ יָשִׁיש עָטוּר תְּפִלִּין פּוֹשֵׁט
יָד רְפוּיָה וּבְעֵינָיו הַשְּׁלֵמָה עִם הַנּוֹרָא מִכֹּל; נַעַר שֶׁנִּסָּה
לְהַבְרִיחַ קְלִפּוֹת שֶׁל תַּפּוּחֵי אֲדָמָה אֶל הַגֶּטוֹ מֻכְתָּר
בִּקְבוּצָה צוֹהֶלֶת שֶׁל אַנְשֵׁי מִשְׁמָר, הַמְלַוִּים בִּצְחוֹק גַּס
אֶת הַפְשָׁטָתוֹ קֹדֶם שֶׁיֻּכֶּה עַד מָוֶת:

13 14 קְבוּצָה שֶׁל צְעִירִים הִתְגּוֹדְדָה לְמוּל לוּחַ מוֹדָעוֹת: אַחַת
15 מֵהֶן, כְּתוּבָה בְּיִידִישׁ, מָשְׁכָה אֶת תְּשׂוּמַת לִבִּי: הַסְבֵּר
לָנוּ שֶׁזּוֹ הוֹדָעָה עַל קוֹנְצֶרְט שֶׁיֵּעָרֵךְ בּוֹ בַּיּוֹם, מַקְהֵלָה
16 קְטַנָּה וְכִנּוֹר בּוֹדֵד; מוֹדָעוֹת אֲחֵרוֹת סִפְּרוּ עַל שִׁעוּרֵי תּוֹרָה
17 וְהַרְצָאוֹת בְּעִנְיְנֵי דְּיוֹמָא: הַאִם הָיָה בְּכוֹחָם שֶׁל אֵלֶּה
לְהַשְׁתִּיק, וְלוּ לְרֶגַע, אֶת הָרָעָב הַמְנַסֵּר אוֹ לַחֲנֹק אֶת
18 הָאֵימָה מִפְּנֵי הֶעָתִיד? מִנַּיִן שָׁאֲבוּ הַיְּהוּדִים אֶת הַכֹּחַ
לְהַבִּיט כָּךְ בְּעֵינָיו שֶׁל הַמַּלְאָךְ הַמַּשְׁחִית?!

19 פָּגַשְׁנוּ גַּם בְּאַנְשֵׁי הַיּוּדְנְרַאט, רָאשֵׁי הַקָּהָל, אֲמְלָלִים אֲשֶׁר
בְּיָדָם הֻפְקְדוּ חַיֵּי אֲחֵיהֶם וְאַחְיוֹתֵיהֶם מִבְּלִי יְכֹלֶת
20 לְהוֹשִׁיעָם: שׁוּב הֻטַּל עֲלֵיהֶם לְאַרְגֵּן טְרַנְסְפּוֹרְט שֶׁל
אֲנָשִׁים, וּמְנוֹעֵי הַמַּשָּׂאִיּוֹת כְּבָר רָעֲמוּ בַּכִּכָּר הַמֶּרְכָּזִית:
21 בִּדְחִיפוֹת וּצְעָקוֹת נִדְחֲקוּ אִמָּהוֹת וְיַלְדֵיהֶן, קְשִׁישִׁים
וּמִשְׁעֲנוֹתֵיהֶם בִּידֵיהֶם, חוֹלִים וְנָכִים וּתְשׁוּשִׁים אֶל פִּיהָ
22 הַפָּעוּר שֶׁל הַמַּשָּׂאִית, וּבְעֵינֵי כֻּלָּם אֵימָה מְסַיֶּטֶת: בְּדַרְכָּן
אֶל תַּחֲנַת הָרַכֶּבֶת הַסְּמוּכָה, הוֹתִירוּ אַחֲרֵיהֶן הַמַּשָּׂאִיּוֹת
זְעָקָה אִלֶּמֶת מְהוּלָה בַּעֲשָׁן שָׁחֹר, וִידִיעָה וַדָּאִית כּוֹאֶבֶת,
כִּי גַּם מָחָר וְגַם מָחֳרָתַיִם יַחֲזֹר מַחֲזֶה זֶה עַל עַצְמוֹ, עַד
נְשִׁימָתוֹ הָאַחֲרוֹנָה שֶׁל הַגֶּטוֹ:

girl, holding tightly her infant sister who was weeping out of hunger listlessly, maybe dying, maybe sleeping; an elder crowned with *tefillin* stretching out a feeble hand, his eyes reflecting the peace he had made with the most dreadful of all; a boy who had tried to smuggle potato skins into the ghetto surrounded by a group of guards reveling with coarse laughter as they stripped him before he was beaten to death.

13　A group of young people was assembled around a
14　bulletin board. One of the announcements, written in
15　Yiddish, drew my attention. It was explained to us that this was an announcement about a concert to be held
16　that very day, a small choir and a violinist. Other announcements told about Torah instruction and
17　lectures on current events. Did these have the power, even if momentary, to silence gnawing hunger or to
18　stifle the dread of what the future held? Whence did this nation draw the strength to stare into the eyes of the destroying angel?!

19　We also met with members of the *Judenrat*, community leaders, those unfortunates into whose hands were entrusted the lives of their brothers and sisters without
20　the power to save them. Once again they were forced to organize people for a *transport*, while the motors of the
21　trucks already were roaring in the central square. With shoving and shouting, mothers and their children were forced – along with the elderly holding their canes, the ailing and the crippled and the feeble – into the cavernous maws of the trucks, and all their eyes were
22　filled with nightmarish terror. On their way to the nearby train depot, the trucks left behind them a silent scream shrouded in black smoke, and the painful certain knowledge that tomorrow and the day after tomorrow this scene would be repeated until the ghetto's last breath.

23 הַחֲזָרָה אֶל רְחוֹבָהּ הָרָאשִׁי שֶׁל הָעִיר, עַל הֲמוֹנָהּ וּשְׁאוֹנָהּ
וּמִסְחָרָהּ וּצְחוֹקָהּ, הֶעֱבִירָה אוֹתִי בְּאַחַת מֵעוֹלָם לְעוֹלָם:

24 גֶּדֶר דַּקִּיקָה וְכַמָּה שְׁעָרִים הִפְרִידוּ בֵּין עוֹלָמוֹת כֹּה שׁוֹנִים:

25 מַה יּוֹדְעִים דָּרֵי הָעוֹלָם הָאֶחָד עַל שְׁכֵנֵיהֶם שֶׁבָּעוֹלָם
הָאַחֵר? וְאִם אֲסַפֵּר – הֲיַקְשִׁיבוּ? וְאִם יַקְשִׁיבוּ? – הֲיוּכְלוּ
לְהַאֲמִין? וְאִם יַאֲמִינוּ – הַאִם לֹא יְנַסּוּ לְהַסְבִּיר אוֹ לְטַהֵר
אֶת מַצְפּוּנָם בִּטְעָמִים שׁוֹנִים וּמְשֻׁנִּים? וּכְשֶׁיִּשְׁאָלוּנִי לָמָה
אֵרַע לַיְּהוּדִים כָּל זֹאת – מָה אָשִׁיב?

23   The return to the city's main street, with its traffic and
     tumult, crowds and carousing, brought me at once from
24   one world to another. A narrow wall and a few gates
25   separated worlds that were so different. What do the
     dwellers of one world know about their neighbors in
     the other one? And if I were to tell, would they listen?
     And if they were to listen, could they believe? And if
     they were to believe, would they not attempt to explain,
     or to cleanse their consciences, with scores of different
     and differing rationalizations? And if they were to ask
     me why all of this befell the Jews, how would I answer?

פרק ג

הַחֹשֶׁךְ הַפָּרוּשׂ עַל הַכֹּל

1 נִכְתַּב עַל דַּף קָרוּעַ שֶׁנִּמְצָא בֵּין שְׁתֵּי מְטוֹת עֵץ:

2 3 גֶרְטְרוּד שְׁמִי: הַרְבֵּה גֶרְטְרוּד הָיוּ בְּעִירֵנוּ, אַךְ בַּצְּרִיף

4 הָאָרֹךְ וְהַקַּר הַזֶּה אֵין עוֹד גֶרְטְרוּד מִלְּבַדִּי: יֵשׁ כָּאן
אָנוּשְׁקָה שֶׁבָּאָה מֵאוּקְרָאִינָה וְגִיטֶל מִפּוֹלִין, הֶלֶנָה
מִגֶרְמַנְיָה וְגְרָאצִיָה מִיָּוֵן, וְעוֹד שׁוּרָה אֲרֻכָּה שֶׁל מִי שֶׁהָיוּ

5 פַּעַם נָשִׁים: אֵיזֶה מַגְנֵט נוֹרָא וּבִלְתִּי מוּחָשׁ שָׁאַב אוֹתָנוּ
מִכָּל קַצְוֵי הַיַּבֶּשֶׁת לְכָאן, וְיָצַק אֶת כֻּלָּנוּ בִּדְמוּת אַחַת:

6 קַבְקַבִּים שֶׁל עֵץ וְשִׂמְלַת בַּד גַּס, שְׂמִיכָה אַחַת לְכַסּוֹת
אֶת גּוּפֵנוּ בַּקַּר שֶׁאֵינוֹ יוֹדֵעַ רַחֵם, וְגַם קְעָרָה שֶׁל פַּח וְכַף
שֶׁמֵּעוֹלָם לֹא הָיָה בָּהֶן כְּדֵי לְהַשְׂבִּיעַ אֶת הָרָעָב הַמְנַקֵּר

7 בְּלֹא הֶרֶף: הֶעָבַר הוֹלֵךְ וּמְטַשְׁטֵשׁ וּבִמְקוֹמוֹ בָּאִים רַק
הַהוֹוֶה, הַיּוֹם, הַשָּׁעָה, הָרֶגַע, מְכוֹנַת הַתְּפִירָה, מְנַת
הַמָּרָק הַדְּלוּחַ, הַמִּסְדָּר שֶׁבּוֹ מִתְמוֹטְטוֹת אֲחָדוֹת מֵאִתָּנוּ
וַאֲחֵרוֹת נִשְׁלָפוֹת מִן הַשּׁוּרָה וְנֶעֱלָמוֹת, כְּשֶׁהֵן מְלֻוּוֹת
בִּצְוָחוֹת וּבִכְלָבִים, וְאִישׁ אֵינוֹ יוֹדֵעַ אֶל אָן:

8 9 הַהֹוֶה מְמַלֵּא אֶת כָּל הֲוָיָתֵנוּ: עַל הֶעָתִיד אֵין אִישׁ
10 מְדַבֵּר, וּבְקֹשִׁי אַזְכֹּר אֶת הֶעָבַר: הוֹי, כַּמָּה שׁוֹטִים וְעִוְרִים
11 הָיִינוּ: אֶת הַהַצָּעָה לַעֲזֹב אֶת הַמּוֹלֶדֶת וְלִהַגֵּר אֶל הַמִּזְרָח
הַנִּדָּח דָּחִינוּ, מִן הַכְּתוּבוֹת "אֵין כְּנִיסָה לִיהוּדִים"
הִתְעַלַּמְנוּ, וְאֶת אָזְנֵינוּ אָטַמְנוּ מִלִּשְׁמֹעַ אֶת נְאוּמֵי

CHAPTER III

THE DARKNESS SPREAD OVER ALL

1 Written upon a scrap of paper found between two wooden beds:

2 3 Gertrude is my name. There were many Gertrudes in our town, but in this long, cold barracks there is no
4 Gertrude but me. There is an Anushka here who comes from the Ukraine, and Gittel from Poland, Helen from Germany, and Gratzia from Greece, and a continuing
5 long list of those who once were women. What cruel, callous magnet drew us here from all corners of the
6 continent, and cast all of us into one mold: wooden shoes and a dress of coarse fabric, a blanket to cover our body in a cold that knows no mercy, and a tin plate and a spoon that never could hold enough to satisfy the
7 incessant gnawing hunger. The past is becoming blurred, replaced only by the present, today, right now, this moment, the sewing machine, a portion of foul soup, the lineup where some of us collapse and from which others are plucked away to disappear, accompanied by shrieks and dogs, and no one knows where.

8 9 The present fills all of our existence. About the future no
10 one speaks, and with difficulty I remember the past. O,
11 how foolish and blind we were! We rejected the advice to abandon the homeland, to emigrate to the distant east, and we hid ourselves from the signs, "No Jews Allowed." Our ears we sealed from hearing the hateful

הַשְּׂטָנָה, שֶׁהֲרֵי רַק מִלִּים הָיוּ, וּמַה כְּבָר יְכוֹלוֹת מִלִּים
לַעֲשׂוֹת? בְּכָל מְאֹדֵנוּ רָצִינוּ לְהַאֲמִין, שֶׁאִם רַק נִכְפֹּף 12
קוֹמָה לִזְמַן קָט, תַּעֲבֹר הַסּוּפָה וְאֵינֶנָּה: גַּם לְאַחַר הַלַּיְלָה 13
שֶׁבּוֹ נִשְׂרְפוּ בָּתֵּי הַכְּנֶסֶת, וְהָרְחוֹבוֹת הוּצְפוּ בִּבְדֹלַח
הַזְּכוּכִיּוֹת הַמְּנֻפָּצוֹת, הִמְשַׁכְנוּ לְקַוּוֹת לְטוֹב, שֶׁהֲרֵי רַע
יוֹתֵר כְּבָר לֹא יוּכַל לִהְיוֹת, וְכֻלָּנוּ אַחֲרֵי הַכֹּל בְּנֵי תַּרְבּוּת
אֲנַחְנוּ:

אוֹי לוֹ לַשּׁוֹטֶה הָעִוֵּר, שֶׁלֹּא יָדַע מַה צוֹפֵן הֶעָתִיד: הָיָה זֶה 14 15
יוֹם שִׁשִּׁי בָּעֶרֶב: יָשַׁבְנוּ בַּסָּלוֹן, וּמְנֻפְרָד, אָבִי הַנָּכֶה בְּכִסֵּא 16
גַּלְגַּלִּים, הִצְטָרֵף לְשִׁירַת הַמַּקְהֵלָה שֶׁהֻשְׁמְעָה בָּרַדְיוֹ: 17
לְפֶתַע נִפְרְצָה הַדֶּלֶת וְהֵם נִכְנְסוּ, שְׁחֹרֵי בֶּגֶד וּמְצֻחְצְחֵי 18
מַגָּף: אֶת אַבָּא דָּחֲפוּ לַחֶדֶר הַסָּמוּךְ וְעָלֵינוּ צִוּוּ לֶאֱרֹז 19
מִזְוָדָה בְּתוֹךְ עֶשֶׂר דַּקּוֹת: "אַתֶּן יוֹצְאוֹת לְמָקוֹם מוּגָן
וּבָטוּחַ", אָמְרוּ, "מַהֵר, מַהֵר!": וּלְאַחַר מִכֵּן רַק תְּמוּנוֹת 20
חֲטוּפוֹת וְקוֹלוֹת מְקֻטָּעִים: יָרֵחַ בּוֹדֵד, מַבָּטֵיהֶם 21
הֶחָלוּלִים שֶׁל הַשְּׁכֵנִים, כִּכַּר הָעִיר הַקְּפוּאָה, זַעֲקַת
הַפְּרֵדָה שֶׁל אִמָּא, הַמַּשָּׂאִית הַמַּצְחִינָה, הָרַכֶּבֶת שֶׁאֵין בָּהּ
טִפַּת אֲוִיר לִנְשִׁימָה, הַצְּרִיף הָאָרֹךְ שֶׁרַק מְטוֹת עֵץ בּוֹ,
וְהַקָּאפוֹ חֲמוּצַת הַפָּנִים:

אֶת שַׂעֲרוֹתֵינוּ גִּלְּחוּ כְּשֶׁהִכְנִיסָנוּ לַצְּרִיף, וּבַמָּקוֹם הַכּוֹכָב 22
הַצָּהֹב הַמְשֻׁשֶּׁה, צָרְבוּ עַל יָדֵינוּ מִסְפָּר כָּחֹל: וּמֵאוֹתוֹ רֶגַע 23
רַק לִתְפֹּר וְלִתְפֹּר, מִבֹּקֶר עַד עֶרֶב, לְלֹא מָנוֹחַ, יוֹם אַחַר
יוֹם, כּוֹבָעִים, מְעִילִים, חֲלָצוֹת וּמִכְנָסַיִם שֶׁיַּתְאִימוּ לַמַּגָּף
הַמְצֻחְצָח: בַּתְּחִלָּה עוֹד שָׁאַלְתִּי "לָמָה?". לָמָה אֲנִי? לָמָה 24

speeches, for they were just words and what can words
12   really accomplish? With all our might we wanted to
believe that if only we would humble ourselves a short
13   while, the storm would pass and be no more. Even after
the night of the burning synagogues, when the streets
were covered with shattered glass, we continued
hoping for the best, since nothing worse could come
to pass and, after all, everyone was cultured there.
14   Alas for the blind fools who did not know what the
15 16 future held. It was on a Friday night. We were sitting in
the salon and my crippled, wheelchair-bound father,
Manfred, was singing along with the choir being
17   broadcast on the radio. Suddenly the door was broken
down and they entered, black uniforms and shining
18   boots. They shoved father into an adjoining room, and
they commanded us to pack a suitcase within ten
19   minutes. "Where you are going is safe and sheltered,"
20   they said. "Hurry! Hurry!" Later, only interrupted
21   images and fragmented sounds: an isolated rifle shot,
the vacant stares of the neighbors, the frozen city
square, a mother's farewell cry, the filthy truck, the
boxcar with not a breath of fresh air, the long barracks
with nothing but wooden beds, and the sour-faced
Kapo.
22   Our hair they shaved when they brought us into the
barracks, and in place of the six-pointed yellow star
23   they burned a blue number into our arms, and from
that moment only sewing and sewing from morning to
night, without rest, day after day, hats, coats, shirts, and
24   trousers appropriate for the shining boots. At first I still

אֲנַחְנוּ? לָמָה עַכְשָׁו? אַךְ חָדַלְתִּי מִלִּשְׁאֹל: הַשְּׁאֵלָה   25
מַכְאִיבָה יוֹתֵר בְּאֵין לָהּ תְּשׁוּבָה:

הַלַּיְלָה יִקְחוּ אֶת כֻּלָּנוּ לְמָקוֹם אַחֵר: כָּךְ סִפְּרָה הַקָּאפּוֹ,   27 26

וְלֹא הוֹסִיפָה דָּבָר, אַךְ פָּנֶיהָ קָדְרוּ: אֲנִי כּוֹתֶבֶת כָּל זֹאת   28

עַל דַּף הַנְּיָר: וְאִם יִמְצָא אוֹתוֹ אֵי פַּעַם בֶּן אֱנוֹשׁ, אוּלַי   29
יִהְיֶה בְּכֹחוֹ לִשְׁאֹל עַל מַה שֶּׁלֹּא

asked "Why?" Why me? Why us? Why now? But I
25 stopped asking. The question is more painful when
there is no answer.

26 27 Tonight they will take all of us to another location. This
is what the Kapo told us, and she did not add another
28 word, but her face was gloomy. I am writing all of this
29 on scraps of paper. And if a human being should ever
find them, perhaps he will have the strength to ask for a
reason why there was no

פרק ד

אֶל מוּל פְּנֵי הַתְּהוֹם

1   מִלּוֹתָיו הָאַחֲרוֹנוֹת שֶׁל יַעֲקֹב דָּוִד בֶּן יוֹאֵל צְבִי הַלֵּוִי:

2 3 אַרְבַּע פְּעָמִים נוֹלַדְתִּי וּפַעַם אַחַת כְּבָר מַתִּי: לָרִאשׁוֹנָה
    נוֹלַדְתִּי לְקוֹל מִצְהֲלוֹת הוֹרַי וּשְׁמוֹנַת אַחַי וְאַחְיוֹתַי
    כְּשֶׁבָּאתִי לָעוֹלָם בְּעֶזְרַת יְיָ יִתְבָּרֵךְ לִפְנֵי עֶשְׂרִים וְחָמֵשׁ

4   שָׁנָה: שָׁלֹשׁ פְּעָמִים נוֹסָפוֹת נוֹלַדְתִּי בְּעֶשֶׂר הַשָּׁנִים
5   הָאַחֲרוֹנוֹת, וּבָהֶן גַּם מַתִּי כְּבָר פַּעַם אֶחָת: אַחֲרֵי הַמָּוֶת
    הַהוּא לֹא יַפְחִיד אוֹתִי עוֹד שׁוּם מָוֶת:

6   בִּשְׁנָיָה נוֹלַדְתִּי בְּלֵיל הַסֶּלֶקְצְיָה, כְּשֶׁאָסְפוּ אוֹתָנוּ, כָּל
7   הַגְּבָרִים שֶׁבָּעֲיָרָה, אֶל הַכִּכָּר הַמֶּרְכָּזִית: הַכּוֹכָבִים
    נִסְתַּלְּקוּ לָהֶם וְרַק הַטָּלַאי הַצָּהֹב הִבְלִיחַ בַּחֲשֵׁכָה:

8   נִדְרַשְׁנוּ לְהִסְתַּדֵּר בְּשׁוּרָה אֲרֻכָּה וְלַחֲשֹׂף אֶת פֶּלֶג גּוּפֵנוּ
9   הָעֶלְיוֹן: בָּזֶה אַחַר זֶה עָבַרְנוּ לְאוֹרָהּ שֶׁל מְנוֹרַת שֶׁמֶן כֵּהָה
    לְיַד שָׂטָן לְבוּשׁ שְׁחוֹרִים, שֶׁהוֹרָה בִּתְנוּעַת יָד לְיָמִין אוֹ

10   לִשְׂמֹאל: מִיָּד הֵבַנְתִּי כִּי לְצַד זֶה זֶה נִשְׁלְחִים הַחֲזָקִים
11   וְהַחֲסוֹנִים וּלְשָׁם הַקְּטַנִּים וְהַזְּקֵנִים: בִּמְהִירוּת מִלֵּאתִי אֶת
    נַעֲלַי בֶּעָפָר וְכָךְ גָּבַהְתִּי בְּכַמָּה סֶנְטִימֶטְרִים, נָפַחְתִּי אֶת
    חָזִי וְאַף צָעַדְתִּי עַל בְּהוֹנוֹתַי בְּעָבְרִי לְיָדוֹ; נִשְׁלַחְתִּי עִם

12   הַחֲסוֹנִים: מֵאַחַר יוֹתֵר שָׁמַעְנוּ אֶת הַיְּרִיּוֹת וְיָדַעְתִּי כִּי חַיַּי
    נִתְּנוּ לִי בְּמַתָּנָה. יִתְבָּרֵךְ שְׁמוֹ:

CHAPTER IV

CONFRONTING THE ABYSS

1   The last words of Yaakov-David Ben Yoel-Tzvi Halevi:

2   Four times was I born, and once already have I died.

3   My first birth was accompanied by the joyful voices of
    my parents and my eight brothers and sisters when I
    came into the world, with the help of God, may He be

4   blessed, twenty-five years ago. I was born three other
    times over the past ten years, during which time I also

5   died once. After that death, no death could ever
    frighten me.

6   The second time, I was born on the night of the
    Selection, when they gathered us, all the males in town,

7   to the central square. The stars had disappeared and

8   only the yellow patches flickered in the darkness. We

9   were told to form a long line and strip to the waist. One
    by one we passed by the light of a dim oil lamp near a
    devil dressed in black who with the wave of a hand

10 directed to the left or to the right. At once I realized that
    the strong and the sturdy were being sent to one side,

11 and the young and the aged to the other. Hastily I filled
    my shoes with dirt, to gain a few centimeters in height.
    Swelling my chest, I even walked on my toes as I

12 passed by him. I was sent with the sturdy. Later we
    heard the shots and I knew that my life had been given
    to me as a gift. Blessed be His name.

בַּשְּׁלִישִׁית נוֹלַדְתִּי כַּאֲשֶׁר נִלְקְחוּ אֶלֶף מֵאִתָּנוּ לִצְעֹד לִפְנֵי 13

הַצָּבָא בִּשְׂדוֹת הַמִּלְחָמָה: הַשֶּׁטַח נִתְמַלֵּא בְּמוֹקְשִׁים רַבִּים 14

וְאָנוּ הָיִינוּ כְּחוֹמָה חַיָּה לִפְנֵי הַמַּחֲנֶה: בְּכָל יוֹם וָיוֹם 15

הִתְמַעֵט מִסְפָּרֵנוּ כְּשֶׁאָנוּ מוֹתִירִים אַחֲרֵינוּ חֲבֵרִים שְׁסוּעִים

לְמַאֲכַל עוֹף הַשָּׁמַיִם וְחַיּוֹת הַיַּעַר: שִׁבְעִים וּשְׁמוֹנָה מֵאִתָּנוּ 16

שָׂרְדוּ אֶת הַמַּסָּע: חַשְׁתִּי כִּי נוֹלַדְנוּ מֵחָדָשׁ כְּשֶׁהִגַּעְנוּ בְּסוֹף 17

הַיּוֹם אֶל הַמַּתְבֵּן שֶׁבּוֹ זָכִינוּ לִמְנַת הַמָּרָק הַדָּלִיל הַיּוֹמִי.

בָּרוּךְ יְיָ יוֹם | יוֹם:

בָּרְבִיעִית נוֹלַדְתִּי עוֹד בְּאוֹתוֹ לַיְלָה: יָצָאתִי לְרֶגַע מִן 19 18

הַמַּתְבֵּן אֶל הֶחָצֵר הָאֲחוֹרִית, וְעוֹד הִסְפַּקְתִּי לִרְאוֹת אֶת

הַגָּפְרוּר הַנִּצָּת וְאֶת הַחִיּוּךְ הַמַּחְלִיא שֶׁל הַמַּצִּית: הַחוֹמָה 20

הַחַיָּה עָשְׂתָה אֶת שֶׁלָּהּ וְשׁוּב אֵין בָּהּ צֹרֶךְ: הַמַּתְבֵּן הֶעֱלָה 21

בָּאֵשׁ וְכָל חֲבֵרַי עָלוּ עַל הַמּוֹקֵד הַשָּׁמַיְמָה, קָרְבָּן עוֹלָה

לֵאלֹהִים יִתְבָּרַךְ:

מִי שֶׁנּוֹלַד אַרְבַּע פְּעָמִים לֹא יָמוּת פַּעַם אַחַת בִּלְבָד: 22

מוֹתִי בָּא עָלַי לְאַחַר שֶׁבָּרַחְתִּי מִמְּקוֹם הַשְּׂרֵפָה, נִתְפַּסְתִּי 23

בִּידֵי מְקוֹמִיִּים וְצֹרְפְתִּי אֶל רַכֶּבֶת שֶׁיָּצְאָה אֶל הָעֲבוֹדָה

הַמְשַׁחְרֶרֶת: תִּזְמֹרֶת קִבְּלָה אֶת פָּנֵינוּ וְכֻלָּנוּ הוּבַלְנוּ, סַבּוֹן 24

וּמַגֶּבֶת בְּיָדֵינוּ, לִשְׁטֹף אֶת גּוּפֵנוּ הַמַּזִּיעַ: רֵיחַ שֶׁל בְּשַׂר 25

שָׂרוּף הִטְרִיף אֶת חוּשֵׁינוּ; הַסַּבּוֹן בָּעַר בְּיָדֵינוּ, וְהַתִּזְמֹרֶת

מְנַגֶּנֶת: בְּרַחֲמֵי הָאֵל עָלַי, נִשְׁלַפְתִּי בָּרֶגַע הָאַחֲרוֹן מִן 26

הַשּׁוּרָה וְלֹא הִצְטָרַפְתִּי אֶל הַהֲמוֹנִים הָעֲרֻמִּים שֶׁנִּדְחֲפוּ

אֶל הַחֶדֶר בִּפְרָאוּת: הַדֶּלֶת נִטְרְקָה בְּרַעַשׁ אַדִּירִים וּמִן 27

הַחֶדֶר בָּקַע קוֹל אֲשֶׁר הַשָּׂפָה אֵינֶנָּה יוֹדַעַת לְתָאֲרוֹ:

שְׁרִיקַת וְרִימָתוֹ שֶׁל גַּז צוֹרֵחַ לְוְתָה בִּבְלִיל שֶׁל "שְׁמַע 28

יִשְׂרָאֵל" וּ"מַאמעלע" "יְיָ אֱלֹהֵינוּ", וּ"מַאדְרִי מִיאָה",

13   The third time I was born when one thousand of us
were taken to walk in front of soldiers on a battlefield.

14   The area was full of mines and we formed a living wall

15   before the troops. Each and every day our number
diminished as comrades ripped apart were left behind
as food for the birds of the heavens and the beasts of the

16 17 field. Seventy-eight of us survived the march. I felt that
our lives began anew when we finally reached the barn
where we were favored with our daily portion of thin
soup. Blessed be the Lord each day.

18 19 The fourth time, I was born later that night. I had left
the barn for the yard behind it, where I managed to
catch sight of a spark from a match and the sickening

20   smile of the one who had lit it. Since the living wall had

21   fulfilled its mission, it was no longer needed. The barn
went up in flames and all my comrades soared
heavenward on the flaming pyre, a sacrificial offering
ascending to God, may He be blessed.

22   Whoever has been born four times will not die only

23   once. My death came to me after I had fled from the site
of the fire. I was captured by locals and forced into a
boxcar on its way to the place where "work makes one

24   free." An orchestra greeted us, and all of us were led,
holding soap and a towel, to wash our sweat-covered

25   bodies. The smell of flesh on fire confused our senses.
The soap seemed to be burning in our hands, and the

26   orchestra was playing. Thanks to God's mercies for me,
I was removed from the line at the last moment, and
did not become part of the naked mass shoved into the

27   room so savagely. The door slammed with a deafening
noise and from the room burst forth sounds that no

28   words can adequately describe: the howling hiss of gas
streaming in accompanied by a mingling of faint and
feeble cries: "*Sh'ma yisrael*" and "*mameleh,*" "the Lord

"יְיָ אֶחָד" וְ"טַאטעלע", צְוָחוֹת דּוֹמְעוֹת וְשׁוֹקְטוֹת וְקוֹל
דְּמָמָה דַקָּה: כָּאן הִתְחִיל תַּפְקִידִי: לְסַלֵּק אֶת הַגּוּפוֹת, 29
לַעֲקֹר אֶת שִׁנֵּי הַזָּהָב, לִדְחֹס אֶת הַמֵּתִים אֶל פִּי הַתַּנּוּר:
כְּשֶׁעֲקַרְתִּי אֶת שִׁנָּיו שֶׁל אָחִי לֵייזֶר, שֶׁלֹּא רְאִיתִיו כַּמָּה 30
שָׁנִים, מֵת לִבִּי בְּקִרְבִּי; גּוּפִי הִמְשִׁיךְ לִחְיוֹת, וַאֲנִי מֵת
מְהַלֵּךְ. יְיָ נָתַן לִי חַיִּים וַיְיָ כְּבָר לְקָחָם, יְהִי שֵׁם יְיָ מְבֹרָךְ:
כַּמָּה עָמַל רִבּוֹנוֹ שֶׁל עוֹלָם כְּדֵי שֶׁנְּאַבֵּד אֶת אֱמוּנָתֵנוּ בּוֹ, 31
אַךְ עַל אַפּוֹ וְעַל חֲמָתוֹ לֹא עָשִׂינוּ זֹאת:
כְּשֶׁאָמוּת בַּפַּעַם הַנּוֹסֶפֶת, אַל תִּקְרְעוּ עָלַי וְאַל תִּתְאַבְּלוּ, 32
שֶׁאֵין מָוֶת אַחַר מָוֶת: אַל תָּהִינוּ גַּם לִשְׁאֹל לָמָּה. מַה 33
שֶּׁלֹּא עָשִׂיתִי אֲנִי אַל יַעֲשׂוּ אֲחֵרִים בִּגְלָלִי:

our God" and "*madre mia,*" "the Lord is One" and
29 "*tateleh,*" followed by a low, murmuring sound. Here
my task began: to remove the bodies, to pull out gold
30 teeth, to shove the dead into the oven. When I pulled
out the teeth of my brother Lazer, whom I had not seen
for years, my heart died within me. My body continued
to live, but I became one of the walking dead. The Lord
gave me life, and the Lord took it away, may the name
31 of the Lord be blessed. How the Master of the Universe
has taken such trouble to ensure that we would lose our
faith in Him! Yet, in spite of His wrath and His rage,
we have refused to succumb.

32 When I die again, tear not your garments; mourn not,
33 for there is no death after death. Do not even attempt to
ask why. What I have not accomplished for myself, let
others not try to accomplish on my behalf.

פרק ה

בַּת קוֹל מְרַחֶפֶת וְאוֹמֶרֶת

[את הפרק כולו יש לקרוא במנגינת "איכה", להוציא הפיסקה האחרונה.]

1 בַּת־קוֹל מִשָּׁמַיִם מְרַחֶפֶת וְאוֹמֶרֶת עַל־אֵלֶּה אֲנִי בוֹכִיָּה:

2 עַל־הוֹרֶיהָ שֶׁל־גֶּרְטְרוּד שֶׁנִּקְרְעוּ זֶה־מִזֶּה בִּפְרָאוּת
קהל: עַל־אֵלֶּה אֲנִי בוֹכִיָּה:

3 עַל־גֶּרְטְרוּד וְאָנוּשְׁקָה וְגִ'יטְל וְהֶלֶנָה וְגְרָאצְיָה, שֶׁכָּלָה כּוֹחָן
בְּמַחֲנוֹת הָעֲבוֹדָה   קהל: עַל־אֵלֶּה אֲנִי בוֹכִיָּה:

4 עַל־אַנְשֵׁי הַיּוּדֶנְרַאט וְעַל־הַקָּאפּוֹ הַיְּהוּדִיָּה שֶׁנִּדְרְשׁוּ
לְמַלֵּא תַפְקִיד שֶׁאֵין אָדָם יָכוֹל לְמַלְּאוֹ
קהל: עַל־אֵלֶּה אֲנִי בוֹכִיָּה:

5 עַל־יַעֲקֹב־דָּוִד בֶּן־יוֹאֵל־צְבִי הַלֵּוִי שֶׁמֵּת פַּעֲמַיִם וְנוֹלַד
אַרְבַּע   קהל: עַל־אֵלֶּה אֲנִי בוֹכִיָּה:

6 עַל־תְּשַׁע־מֵאוֹת עֶשְׂרִים־וּשְׁנַיִם חֲבֵרָיו שֶׁעָלוּ הַשָּׁמַיְמָה
בִּשְׂדוֹת הַמּוֹקְשִׁים   קהל: עַל־אֵלֶּה אֲנִי בוֹכִיָּה:

7 עַל־שִׁבְעִים וְשִׁבְעָה הַנִּצּוֹלִים שֶׁאֶפְרָם צָבוּר בְּמַתְבֵּן
קהל: עַל־אֵלֶּה אֲנִי בוֹכִיָּה:

8 עַל־לֵייזֶר שֶׁאַף בַּמְּזָוֶויעִים שֶׁבַּחֲלוֹמוֹתָיו לֹא רָאָה אֶת־
אָחִיו עוֹקֵר אֶת־שְׁנֵי הַזָּהָב מִגּוּפָתוֹ
קהל: עַל־אֵלֶּה אֲנִי בוֹכִיָּה:

9 עַל־אֵלֶּה אֲנִי בוֹכִיָּה וְעַל־הַמִּילְיוֹנִים הַדְּחוּקִים בַּגֶּטָאוֹת

10 וּבְמַחֲנוֹת הַמַּעֲבָר: עַל־הַמְּשׁוֹטְטִים בַּיְּעָרוֹת וְעַל־
הַמִּסְתַּתְּרִים בַּמַּרְתֵּפִים וּבְכוּכִים עַל־מִי שֶׁמָּצָא מִקְלָט

CHAPTER V

A HEAVENLY VOICE, HOVERING, CRIES OUT

[This chapter, except for the final passage, is chanted in the mode of *Eikhah*.]

1 A heavenly voice cries out: For these do I weep.

2 For Gertrude's parents, who were torn away from each other   *Congregation:* For these do I weep.

3 For Gertrude and Anushka, Gittel, Helen, and Gratzia, whose vitality came to an end in labor camps

Congregation: For these do I weep.

4 For members of the *Judenrat* and for the Jewish Kapo, who were asked to fulfill a task that no human being could fulfill   *Congregation:* For these do I weep.

5 For Yaakov-David ben Yoel-Tzvi Halevi who died twice and was born four times

Congregation: For these do I weep.

6 For nine hundred and twenty-two comrades who from mine fields ascended the heavens

Congregation: For these do I weep.

7 For the seventy-seven who were saved, whose dust was gathered in the barn   *Congregation:* For these do I weep.

8 For Lazer, who in his most terrifying nightmares never saw his brother pulling gold teeth from his corpse

Congregation: For these do I weep.

9   For these do I weep, and for the millions crowded in
10 ghettos and in detention camps; for those wandering in forests and those hidden in attics and in underground bunkers, for those who found refuge in the bosom of

בְּחֵיק דָּת־אַחֶרֶת אוֹ אִבֵּד אֶת אֶת־אֱלֹהָיו: עַל־מִי שֶׁנִּתַּן 11
לְנִסּוּיִים בִּידֵי חַיּוֹת־טֶרֶף שֶׁשֵּׁם רוֹפֵא וּמַדְעָן נִקְרָא עֲלֵיהֶן:

עַל־מִי שֶׁמֵּת בָּרָעָב וּבַצָּמָא נֶחְנַק לַמָּוֶת בְּרַכֶּבֶת מַשָּׂא אוֹ 12

בְּתָאֵי הַגַּזִים נִקְבַּר חַי אוֹ נִשְׂרָף: עַל־מִי שֶׁהוּצָא 13
לְהוֹרֵג בִּתְלִיָּה לְמַעַן יִרְאוּ וְיִירָאוּ עַל־מְקַדְּשֵׁי שֵׁם־שָׁמַיִם
וְשֵׁם יִשְׂרָאֵל שֶׁסֵּרְבוּ לְהִכָּנַע וְנִלְחֲמוּ עַד־מָוֶת עַל־מִי
שֶׁאִבַּד אֶת־בֵּיתוֹ וּכְבוֹדוֹ וְתִקְוָתוֹ: עַל־מִי שֶׁנּוֹתַר בַּחַיִּים 14
לַחְיוֹת אֶת־הַזְּוָעָה מֵחָדָשׁ יוֹם | יוֹם | וָרֶגַע | רֶגַע:

עַל־אֵלֶּה אֲנִי בּוֹכִיָּה עַל־עוֹלָלִים שֶׁלֹּא לָמְדוּ לַהֲגוֹת 15
"אִמָּא" עַל־יְלָדִים וִילָדוֹת שֶׁנְּעוּרֵיהֶם נִגְזְלוּ מֵהֶם וְהֵם
קָמְלוּ טֶרֶם פְּרִיחָה: עַל־עֲלָמִים וַעֲלָמוֹת שֶׁלֹּא נִתְבָּרְכוּ 16
מִתַּחַת לַחֻפָּה עַל־זְקֵנִים שֶׁלֹּא זָכוּ לְשֵׂיבָה שֶׁל־חֶסֶד:

עַל־הַתִּזְמוֹרוֹת וְעַל־הַמּוּזִיקָה וְעַל־כָּל־יְפִי הָעוֹלָם 17
שֶׁאָבְדָה לוֹ צִבְעוֹנִיּוּתוֹ וְכֻלּוֹ רַק־חוּם וָאֵפֶר וְשָׁחֹר
עַל־כָּל־אֵלֶּה אֲנִי בּוֹכִיָּה:

כַּמָּה הִתְחַבַּטְתִּי לִפְנֵי הַפַּרְגּוֹד לִפְנֵי חַנּוּן וְרַחוּם רַב חֶסֶד 18
וֶאֱמֶת, בִּקַּשְׁתִּי וְהִתְחַנַּנְתִּי וְרָצִיתִי לְהָבִין: הַאִם נוֹדַע 19
הַדָּבָר בַּמְּרוֹמִים? הֲכָךְ גָּזַר אֵל מָלֵא רַחֲמִים? זוֹ אִמָּה וְזוֹ
שְׁכָרָהּ? וְהִנֵּה, אֵין קוֹל וְאֵין עוֹנֶה, רַק דְּמָמָה זְעוּפָה: יוֹשֵׁב 20 21
בְּסֵתֶר עֶלְיוֹן וּבְצֵל הַדְּמָמָה יִתְלוֹנָן: עֲמֻקִּים וְנִסְתָּרִים 22
וְנוֹרָאִים הֵם הַדְּבָרִים; אִישׁ לֹא יְבִינֵם, גַּם לֹא בְּנוֹת קוֹל
מִשָּׁמַיִם:

11   another faith or who lost their God; for those who were given over to experiments at the hands of wild beasts
12   called doctors and scientists; for those who died of hunger and of thirst, smothered to death in freight trains or in gas chambers, shot, buried alive or
13   cremated; for those who were brought out to be killed by hanging so that they would be seen, and for those who sanctified God's name and the name of the people Israel, refusing to be subdued, fighting to the death. For those who lost their homes, their dignity, and their
14   hope, and for those left alive to live the horror anew, day after day, moment after moment.
15   For these do I weep, for infants who never learned to say "Mommy," for boys and girls whose youth was stolen from them, who withered before coming to
16   blossom; for young men and women who never were blessed beneath the wedding canopy, for the elderly
17   denied the privilege of a gracious old age; for the orchestras and for the music, and for all the world's beauty whose rainbow of colors was lost, replaced by only brown and gray and black. For all these do I weep.
18   I struggled so hard before the veiled curtain, before the merciful and gracious One, of great kindness and truth. How I pled and how I begged, how I wanted to
19   understand. Was all of this known on high? Was this the decree of God who is filled with compassion? This
20   was the reward of such a nation? But there was no sound and no response, only an exasperating silence.
21   The Most High abides in secret, God dwells in the
22   shadow of silence. Deep, hidden, and awesome are the events; no one understands them, not even echoes of the heavenly voice.

פרק ו

עוֹד יְהִי אוֹר

1 שָׁב וְאָמַר כּוֹתֵב דִּבְרֵי הַיָּמִים:

2 בְּפַאֲתֵי הַלַּיְלָה נִכְּרוּ נְגוֹהוֹת רִאשׁוֹנִים שֶׁל קַרְנֵי הַשַּׁחַר:

3 אֵלּוּ הֵאִירוּ עַל שְׂרִידֵי אָדָם בְּבִגְדֵי פַּסִּים שֶׁבָּהוּ עַל

4 סְבִיבוֹתֵיהֶם בְּעֵינַיִם מֵתוֹת: כְּבָר שָׁכְחוּ אֵיךְ לִשְׂמֹחַ וְגוּפָם

5 דָּחָה אֶת הָאֹכֶל שֶׁהֻצַּע לָהֶם: הַחְפוֹרִים סִלְּקוּ אֶל בּוֹרוֹת
עֲנָק אַלְפֵי גְוִיּוֹת עֲרֻמּוֹת וְדַקִּיקוֹת, שֶׁנָּפְלוּ זוֹ עַל גַּבֵּי זוֹ
בְּרִפְיוֹן אֵיבָרִים:

6 בְּמַחֲנוֹת שֶׁל עֲקוּרִים סָבְבוּ כַּוָּרוֹת שֶׁל נְחִילֵי אָדָם, כְּשֶׁהֵם
מְחַפְּשִׂים נוֹאָשׁוֹת אֶת בְּנֵי מִשְׁפְּחוֹתֵיהֶם, וַהֲרֵי הֵם פּוֹחֲדִים
לִקְווֹת פֶּן תִּכָּזֵב תִּקְוָתָם: אֻמְלָלִים שֶׁנִּסּוּ לָשׁוּב אֶל

7 בָּתֵּיהֶם מָצְאוּ בָּהֶם גַּם שְׁכֵנִים עוֹיְנִים, וְלֹא פַעַם נִצְּלוּ רַק

8 בְּנֵס מֵהֶרֶג אַחַר הֶרֶג: אֲנָשִׁים אֲשֶׁר לֹא יָדְעוּ אוֹ אֲשֶׁר
בִּקְשׁוּ לֹא לָדַעַת, אֲשֶׁר סֵרְבוּ לְהַאֲמִין אוֹ אֲשֶׁר אָסְרוּ
לְהַאֲמִין, עָמְדוּ בְּעֵינַיִם קְרוּעוֹת וְלֹא יָדְעוּ לְאָן יַפְנוּ אֶת
מַבָּטָם וְכֵיצַד יְטַהֲרוּ אֶת מַצְפּוּנָם:

9 אַךְ אַט אַט שָׁבוּ אֲנָשִׁים לְבָתֵּיהֶם וּבְנֵי מִשְׁפָּחָה הִתְאַחֲדוּ;

10 אֲנָשִׁים שָׁבוּ וְנָשְׂאוּ וְיִלָּדִים נוֹלָדוּ: גַּלִּים אַחַר גַּלִּים שָׁטְפוּ
הַנִּצּוֹלִים אֶל הַמִּזְרָח, מְדִינָה גֵּאָה קָמָה וּמֶרְכְּזֵי יַהֲדוּת

11 פּוֹרְחִים בְּרַחֲבֵי תֵבֵל: רַכָּבוֹת שׁוּב נוֹסְעוֹת אֶל אַתְרֵי

CHAPTER VI

LET THERE BE LIGHT AGAIN

1   Again did the chronicler speak:

2   At the edges of the night, the first rays of dawn could be

3   discerned. They shone upon the remnants of human beings in striped clothing who stared at their surround-

4   ings with dead eyes. They have forgotten how to be happy, and their bodies reject any food offered them.

5   Bulldozers thrust into gigantic pits thousands of thin, naked corpses that fall, one atop the other, their limbs withered.

6   In camps of the uprooted circled human streams, searching in despair for members of their families,

7   and they were afraid to hope lest their hope be lost. The unfortunates who tried to return to their homes found in them hostile neighbors from time to time, and more than once they were saved only by a miracle from

8   murder following murder. People who did not know or who had sought not to know, who refused to believe or who forbade believing, stood with tearful eyes, not knowing where to direct their gaze or how to cleanse their conscience.

9   Slowly, slowly, people returned to their homes, and family members were reunited. People married again,

10 and children were born. Wave upon wave poured into the East and the State of Israel arose, and centers of

11 Jewish life flourished throughout the world. Trains traveled to resorts once again, and orchestras were

הַנֶּפֶשׁ וְתִזְמוֹרוֹת צוֹהֲלוֹת בְּכָל קַצְוֵי הָאָרֶץ: וּמִי יוֹדֵעַ, 12
אוּלַי כָּךְ בִּקְשׁוּ מִן הַשָּׁמַיִם שֶׁתִּמָּצֵא לָאֲבֵלִים וְלַסּוֹבְלִים
נֶחָמַת מָה:

גִּלּוּיֵי גְּבוּרָה שֶׁל עַזֵּי הַנֶּפֶשׁ הֶעֱלוּ עַל נֵס וְ"קַדִּישׁ" נֶאֱמַר 13
עַל הַמֵּתִים, סִפְרֵי זִכְרוֹנוֹת נִכְתְּבוּ וְאַנְדַּרְטָאוֹת הוּקְמוּ,
וְלָאֲבֵלִים נִמְצָא סוֹף סוֹף מָקוֹם לִבְכּוֹת בּוֹ אֶת מֵתֵיהֶם:

פּוֹשְׁעִים בָּאוּ עַל עָנְשָׁם, נְכֵי גוּף אוֹ נֶפֶשׁ זָכוּ לְעֶזְרָה, אַךְ 14
בְּכָל אֵלֶּה לֹא הָיָה כְּדֵי לְכַבֵּל אֶת מַלְאַךְ הַחֲלוֹמוֹת,
הַמַּמְשִׁיךְ לְהַבְעִית אֶת הַנִּצּוֹלִים לַיְלָה אַחַר לַיְלָה, וְלֹא
כְּדֵי לְהַשְׁתִּיק אֶת קוֹל הַמַּצְפּוּן, הַמְנַקֵּר וְתוֹבֵעַ הֶסְבֵּר
לְרִשְׁעוּת הַשְּׂטָנִית וּלְאַטִימוּת הַלֵּב: וּשְׁלַל הַשְּׁאֵלוֹת – 15
רִבּוֹנוֹ שֶׁל עוֹלָם, לָמָה? לָמָה? לָמָה דַּוְקָא אֲנַחְנוּ? לָמָה
דַּוְקָא הֵם? לָמָה עַכְשָׁו? לָמָה כָּךְ? – נוֹתְרוּ תְּלוּיוֹת בַּחֲלָלוֹ
שֶׁל עוֹלָם, מְרַחֲפוֹת מֵעַל כָּל מַעֲשֵׂי אֱנוֹשׁ, וּמַעֲנֶה – אַיִן:

יָמִים יַגִּידוּ מַה לְּמַדְנוּ; רַק הַזְּמַן יְגַלֶּה אִם הִקְשַׁבְנוּ בֶּאֱמֶת 16
לְקוֹלוֹ שֶׁל דַּם הַנִּרְצָחִים הַצּוֹעֵק אֵלֵינוּ מִן הָאֲדָמָה:

אַל תִּתְאַבְּלוּ יוֹתֵר מִדַּי, אַךְ אַל תִּשְׁקְעוּ בְּשִׁכְחָה 17
שֶׁל אֲדִישׁוּת; אַל תַּנִּיחוּ לִימֵי הַחֹשֶׁךְ שֶׁיָּשׁוּבוּ,
בְּכוּ וְגַם מְחוּ אֶת הַדִּמְעָה; אַל תִּמְחֲלוּ
וְאַל תִּסְלְחוּ, אַל תְּנַסּוּ לְהָבִין;
לִמְדוּ לִחְיוֹת לְלֹא מַעֲנֶה:
בְּדָמֵינוּ חָיוּ! 18

12   making joyous music in all corners of the land. Perhaps this is the way in which Heaven sought some consolation for those who suffered and mourned.

13   The heroism of courageous resisters was revealed and proclaimed, and Mourner's Kaddish was recited for the dead, memorial books were written, monuments were erected so that finally mourners could find a place

14   where they could weep for their dead, criminals were punished, and those who were afflicted in body or soul received help. Nevertheless, it was impossible to restrain the angel of dreams who continues to terrify the rescued night after night, impossible to silence the gnawing voice of conscience, which demands an explanation for satanic evil, and for apathetic hearts.

15   Such questions "Why, God, why? Why us? Why them? Why now? Why in that way?" are left suspended in midair, hovering over all human deeds, and there is no response.

16   Time will tell what we have learned; only time will reveal whether we truly have listened to the voice of the blood of the slaughtered crying out from the earth.

17   Do not mourn too much, but do not sink into the forgetfulness of apathy. Do not allow days of darkness to return; weep, but wipe the tears away.
Do not absolve and do not exonerate,
do not attempt to understand.
Learn to live without
an answer.

18   Through our blood, live!

יִזְכּוֹר לְיוֹם הַזִּכָּרוֹן לַשּׁוֹאָה וְלַמֶּרֶד

נִזְכֹּר אֶת אַחֵינוּ וְאֶת אַחְיוֹתֵינוּ,

אֶת בָּתֵּי הָעִיר וְאֶת בָּתֵּי הַכְּפָר,

אֶת רְחוֹבוֹת הָעֲיָרָה שֶׁסָּאֲנוּ כִּנְהָרוֹת

וְאֶת הַפֻּנְדָּק הַבּוֹדֵד עֲלֵי אֹרַח:

אֶת הַיָּשִׁישׁ בְּקַלְסְתֵּר פָּנָיו,

אֶת הָאֵם בְּסוּדָרָהּ,

אֶת הַנַּעֲרָה בְּצַמּוֹתֶיהָ

אֶת הַטַּף;

אֶת אַלְפֵי קְהִלּוֹת יִשְׂרָאֵל

עַל מִשְׁפְּחוֹת הָאָדָם,

אֶת כָּל עֲדַת הַיְּהוּדִים

אֲשֶׁר הֻכְרְעָה לַטֶּבַח עַל אַדְמַת אֵירוֹפָּה

מִידֵי הַכּוֹרֵת הַנָּאצִי;

אֶת הָאִישׁ שֶׁזָּעַק פִּתְאֹם

וּבְזַעֲקָתוֹ מֵת;

אֶת הָאִשָּׁה שֶׁחָבְקָה תִּינוֹקָהּ אֶל לִבָּהּ

וּזְרוֹעוֹתֶיהָ צָנְחוּ;

אֶת הַתִּינוֹק שֶׁאֶצְבְּעוֹתָיו מְגַשְׁשׁוֹת אֶל פִּטְמַת הָאֵם

וְהִיא כְּחוּלָה וְצוֹנֶנֶת;

Yizkor for Yom Hashoah

We shall remember our brothers and our sisters,

the city houses and the country houses,

the *shtetl* streets rushing like rivers

and the lonely inn on the country road —

the aged man and the features of his face,

the mother in her kerchief,

the young girl with her braids,

the child,

the people Israel in thousands of communities

among all the human families,

the entire assembly of Jews

brought down to slaughter on the soil of Europe

by the Nazi destroyer,

the man who suddenly screamed

and while screaming died,

the woman, clutching her infant to her breast,

whose arms gave out,

the infant groping for his mother's nipple

that was blue and cold,

אֶת הָרַגְלַיִם,

אֶת הָרַגְלַיִם שֶׁבִּקְשׁוּ מִפְלָט

וְלֹא הָיָה מָנוֹס עוֹד;

וְאֶת שֶׁקָּפְצוּ יְדֵיהֶם לְאֶגְרוֹף

הָאֶגְרוֹף שֶׁחָפַן אֶת הַבַּרְזֶל,

הַבַּרְזֶל שֶׁהָיָה לְנֶשֶׁק הֶחָזוֹן,

הַיֵּאוּשׁ וְהַמֶּרֶד,

וְהֵם בָּרֵי הַלֵּבָב

וְהֵם פְּקוּחֵי הָעֵינַיִם

וְהֵם שֶׁהִשְׁלִיכוּ נַפְשָׁם מִנֶּגֶד

וְיָדָם קָצְרָה מִלְּהוֹשִׁיעַ;

נִזְכֹּר אֶת הַיּוֹם,

אֶת הַיּוֹם בְּצָהֳרָיו, אֶת הַשֶּׁמֶשׁ שֶׁעָלְתָה

עַל מוֹקֵד הַדָּמִים,

אֶת הַשָּׁמַיִם שֶׁעָמְדוּ גְּבוֹהִים וּמַחֲרִישִׁים;

נִזְכֹּר אֶת תִּלֵּי הָאֵפֶר

אֲשֶׁר מִתַּחַת לַגַּנִּים הַפּוֹרְחִים.

יִזְכֹּר הַחַי אֶת מֵתָיו

כִּי הִנֵּה הֵם מִנֶּגֶד לָנוּ

הִנֵּה נְבָטוֹת עֵינֵיהֶם סָבִיב־סָבִיב

וְאַל דֳּמִי, אַל דֳּמִי לָנוּ,

עֲדֵי יִהְיוּ חַיֵּינוּ רְאוּיִים לְזָכְרָם.

אבא קובנר

the feet,

the feet that sought refuge

though flight was no longer possible,

and those who made their hands into a fist,

the fist that gripped the iron,

the iron that became the weapon of vision,

of despair, and of rebellion,

and those, the pure of heart,

those whose eyes were opened,

those who risked their lives,

though they lacked the power to triumph.

We shall remember the day,

the day in its brightness, the sun that rose

over the bloody conflagration,

the lofty, silent heavens.

We shall remember the mounds of dust

beneath the gardens in bloom.

The living shall remember their dead

for they are forever before us.

Look! Their eyes dart round and about,

allowing us no peace, no peace

until our lives become worthy of their memory.

Abba Kovner, translated by Jules Harlow

אֵל מָלֵא רַחֲמִים שׁוֹכֵן בַּמְּרוֹמִים. הַמְצֵא מְנוּחָה נְכוֹנָה
תַּחַת כַּנְפֵי הַשְּׁכִינָה. בְּמַעֲלוֹת קְדוֹשִׁים וּטְהוֹרִים כְּזֹהַר הָרָקִיעַ
מַזְהִירִים אֶת נִשְׁמוֹת כָּל אַחֵינוּ בְּנֵי יִשְׂרָאֵל שֶׁנִּטְבְּחוּ בַּשּׁוֹאָה,
אֲנָשִׁים נָשִׁים וָטַף, שֶׁנֶּחְנְקוּ וְשֶׁנִּשְׂרְפוּ וְשֶׁנֶּהֶרְגוּ, שֶׁמָּסְרוּ אֶת
נַפְשָׁם עַל קְדוּשׁ הַשֵּׁם, בְּגַן עֵדֶן תְּהֵא מְנוּחָתָם. אָנָּא בַּעַל
הָרַחֲמִים, הַסְתִּירֵם בְּסֵתֶר כְּנָפֶיךָ לְעוֹלָמִים, וּצְרוֹר בִּצְרוֹר
הַחַיִּים אֶת נִשְׁמוֹתֵיהֶם, יְיָ הוּא נַחֲלָתָם, וְיָנוּחוּ בְּשָׁלוֹם עַל
מִשְׁכְּבוֹתֵיהֶם. וְנֹאמַר אָמֵן.

קַדִּישׁ יָתוֹם

יִתְגַּדַּל וְיִתְקַדַּשׁ שְׁמֵהּ רַבָּא,

בְּעָלְמָא דִּי בְרָא כִרְעוּתֵהּ וְיַמְלִיךְ מַלְכוּתֵהּ.

בְּחַיֵּיכוֹן וּבְיוֹמֵיכוֹן וּבְחַיֵּי דְכָל בֵּית יִשְׂרָאֵל

בַּעֲגָלָא וּבִזְמַן קָרִיב, וְאִמְרוּ אָמֵן:

יְהֵא שְׁמֵהּ רַבָּא מְבָרַךְ לְעָלַם וּלְעָלְמֵי עָלְמַיָּא:

יִתְבָּרַךְ וְיִשְׁתַּבַּח וְיִתְפָּאַר וְיִתְרוֹמַם וְיִתְנַשֵּׂא

וְיִתְהַדָּר וְיִתְעַלֶּה וְיִתְהַלָּל שְׁמֵהּ דְּקֻדְשָׁא בְּרִיךְ הוּא.

לְעֵלָּא מִן כָּל בִּרְכָתָא וְשִׁירָתָא

תֻּשְׁבְּחָתָא וְנֶחֱמָתָא דַּאֲמִירָן בְּעָלְמָא, וְאִמְרוּ אָמֵן:

יְהֵא שְׁלָמָא רַבָּא מִן שְׁמַיָּא וְחַיִּים עָלֵינוּ וְעַל כָּל יִשְׂרָאֵל,

וְאִמְרוּ אָמֵן:

עוֹשֶׂה שָׁלוֹם בִּמְרוֹמָיו הוּא יַעֲשֶׂה שָׁלוֹם עָלֵינוּ וְעַל כָּל

יִשְׂרָאֵל, וְאִמְרוּ אָמֵן:

EXALTED, COMPASSIONATE GOD, grant infinite rest in Your sheltering presence, among the holy and pure, to the souls of our brethren who perished in the Shoah – men, women, and children of the House of Israel who were slaughtered, suffocated and burned to ashes. May their memory endure and inspire deeds of charity and goodness in our lives. May their souls thus be bound up in the bond of life. May they rest in peace. And let us say: Amen.

MOURNER'S KADDISH

Yitgadal v'yitkadash sh'mei raba,

b'alma di'vr'a khir'utei, v'yamlikh malkhutei

b'hayeikhon u-v'yomeikhon u-v'hayei d'khol beit Yisrael,

ba'agala u-vi-z'man kariv, v'imru amen.

Y'hei sh'mei raba m'vorakh l'alam u-l'almei almaya.

Yitbarakh v'yishtabah v'yitpa-ar v'yitromam v'yitnasei,

v'yit-hadar v'yit'aleh v'yithalal sh'mei d'kudsha, b'rikh hu,

l'ela min kol birkhata v'shirata

tushb'hata v'nehamata da'amiran b'alma, v'imru amen.

Y'hei sh'lama rabba min sh'maya, v'hayim aleinu v'al kol Yisra'el, v'imru amen.

Oseh shalom bi-m'romav, hu ya'aseh shalom, aleinu v'al kol Yisra-el, v'imru amen.

אונדזער שטעטל ברענט

ס׳ברענט! ברידערלעך, ס׳ברענט!

אוי אונדזער אָרעם שטעטל נעבעך ברענט!

בייזע ווינטן מיט ירגזון

רייסן, ברעכן און צעבלאָזן

שטאַרקער נאָך די ווילדע פלאַמען,

אַלץ אַרום שוין ברענט!

און איר שטייט און קוקט אַזוי זיך

מיט פאַרלייגטע הענט,

און איר שטייט און קוקט אַזוי זיך -

אונדזער שטעטל ברענט!

מרדכי גבירטיג

Undzer Shtetl Brent

S'brent, briderlech s'brent!
Oi unzer orem shtetl nebech brent
Beize vintn mit yirgozun
Reisn brechn un tzeblozn
Shtarker noch di vilde flamen
Altz arum shoin brent
Un ir shteit un kukt azoi zich
Mit farleigte hent
Un ir shteit un kukt azoi zich
Unzer shtetl brent!

It is burning, dear brothers, it is burning!
Our poor little town is burning!
Angry winds whip the flames.
Everything is on fire!
And you stand helplessly
With folded hands and stare
While the flames grow higher
And our little town burns.

Mordechai Gebirtig

זאָג ניט קיין מאָל

זאָג ניט קיין מאָל, אַז דו גייסט דעם לעצטן וועג,
כאָטש הימלען בלייענע פאַרשטעלן בלויע טעג,
קומען וועט נאָך אונדזער אויסגעבענקטע שעה,
ס׳וועט אַ פויק טאָן אונדזער טראָט - מיר זיינען דאָ !

פון גרינעם פּאַלמענלאַנד ביז ווייטן לאַנד פון שניי,
מיר קומען אָן מיט אונדזער פּיין, מיט אונדזער וויי,
און ווו געפאַלן ס׳איז אַ שפּריץ פון אונדזער בלוט,
שפּראָצן וועט דאָרט אונדזער גבורה, אונדזער מוט.

ס׳וועט די מאָרגנזון באַגילדן אונדז דעם היינט,
און דער נעכטן וועט פאַרשווינדן מיטן פיינט
נאָר אויב פאַרזאַמען וועט די זון אין דעם קאַיאָר -
ווי אַ פּאַראָל זאָל גיין דאָס ליד פון דור צו דור.

דאָס ליד געשריבן איז מיט בלוט און ניט מיט בליי,
ס׳איז ניט קיין לידל פון אַ פויגל אויף דער פריי,
דאָס האָט אַ פאָלק צווישן פאַלנדיקע ווענט
דאָס ליד געזונגען מיט נאַגאַנעס אין די הענט.

טאָ זאָג ניט קיין מאָל, אַז דו גייסט דעם לעצטן וועג,
כאָטש הימלען בלייענע פאַרשטעלן בלויע טעג,
קומען וועט נאָך אונדזער אויסגעבענקטע שעה,
עס וועט אַ פויק טאָן אונדזער טראָט - מיר זיינען דאָ !

הירש גליק

Zog Nit Keyn Mol

Never say that there is only death for you
Though leaden skies may be concealing days of blue
Because the hour we have hungered for is near;
Beneath our tread the earth shall tremble: We are here!

From land of palm-tree to the far-off land of snow
We shall be coming with our torment and our woe,
And everywhere our blood has sunk into the earth
Shall our bravery, our vigor blossom forth!

We'll have the morning sun to set our day aglow,
And all our yesterdays shall vanish with the foe,
And if the time is long before the sun appears,
Then let this song go like a signal through the years.

This song was written with our blood and not with lead;
It's not a song that birds sing overhead.
It was a people, among toppling barricades,
That sang this song of ours with pistols and grenades.

So never say that there is only death for you.
For leaden skies may be concealing days of blue
Yet the hour we have hungered for is near;
Beneath our tread the earth shall tremble: We are here!

Hirsh Glick, translated by Aaron Kramer

הַתִּקְוָה

כָּל עוֹד בַּלֵּבָב פְּנִימָה

נֶפֶשׁ יְהוּדִי הוֹמִיָּה

וּלְפַאֲתֵי מִזְרָח קָדִימָה

עַיִן לְצִיּוֹן צוֹפִיָּה

עוֹד לֹא אָבְדָה תִּקְוָתֵנוּ

הַתִּקְוָה בַּת שְׁנוֹת אַלְפַּיִם

לִהְיוֹת עַם חָפְשִׁי בְּאַרְצֵנוּ

אֶרֶץ צִיּוֹן וִירוּשָׁלָיִם.

HATIKVAH

Kol ode balevav penimah

Nefesh yehudi homiyah

Ulfa'atay mizrach kadimah

Ayin l'tzion tzofiah

Ode lo avdah tikvateynu

Hatikvah bat shnot alpayim

Lihiyot am hofshi be-artzaynu

Eretz tzion viyirushalayim.

The Rabbinical Assembly, founded in 1901 and located in New York City, is the international association of Conservative/ Masorti rabbis. The Assembly actively promotes the cause of Conservative/Masorti Judaism and works unceasingly to benefit *Klal Yisrael*; publishes learned texts, prayerbooks and works of Jewish interest; and administers the work of the Committee on Jewish Law and Standards which serves as the halakhic guide for the Conservative Movement. It serves the professional and personal needs of its membership through publications, conferences and benefit programs, and administers the Movement's Joint Placement Commission. Rabbis of the Assembly serve throughout the world, in congregations, on the campus, as educators, hospital and military chaplains, teachers of Judaica, and officers of communal service organizations.

The Rabbinical Assembly
3080 Broadway, New York, New York, 10027
Tel: 212-280-6000, Fax: 212-749-9166
Email: info@rabbinicalassembly.org   www.rabassembly.org

The Schechter Institute of Jewish Studies, Inc. is a non-profit organization which supports a learning community established in Jerusalem in 1984 including: the Schechter Institute of Jewish Studies: A Graduate School for Israeli Educators, where over 450 students learn Jewish studies within a pluralistic environment; The Schechter Center of Jewish Studies: A Rabbinical School for Conservative/Masorti Judaism; The TALI Education Fund which provides Jewish studies programs for 22,000 Israeli children in over 120 state schools and kindergartens; Midreshet Yerushalayim outreach activities for Russian immigrants and for Jewish communities in the Ukraine and Hungary; and Applied Research Institutes in Halakhah, Women in Jewish Law, and Judaism and the Arts. All of these programs advance the struggle for Jewish knowledge, religious pluralism and tolerance in Israel and throughout the world.

Schechter Institute of Jewish Studies, Inc.
475 Riverside Drive, Suite 244, New York, New York, 10115
Tel: 212-870-3173, Fax: 212-870-3176
Email: schechter@jtsa.edu   www.schechter.edu